Going Pro with Pro Tools® 8

Mark I. Altin

Course Technology PTR
A part of Cengage Learning

COURSE TECHNOLOGY
CENGAGE Learning™

Australia • Brazil • Japan • Korea • Mexico • Singapore • Spain • United Kingdom • United States

Going Pro with Pro Tools® 8

Mark I. Altin

Publisher and General Manager,
  Course Technology PTR:
  Stacy L. Hiquet

Associate Director of Marketing:
  Sarah Panella

Manager of Editorial Services:
  Heather Talbot

Marketing Manager: Mark Hughes

Executive Editor: Mark Garvey

Project/Copy Editor: Kezia Endsley

Technical Editor: Eric Kuehnl

Interior Layout Tech: MPS Ltd,
  A Macmillan Company

Cover Designer: Mike Tanamachi

Proofreader: Gene Redding

Indexer: Sharon Shock

For product information and technology assistance, contact us at **Cengage Learning Customer & Sales Support, 1-800-354-9706**

For permission to use material from this text or product, submit all requests online at **cengage.com/permissions**

Further permissions questions can be emailed to **permissionrequest@cengage.com**

Library of Congress Control Number: 2009924531

ISBN-13: 978-1-5986-3947-6
ISBN-10: 1-5986-3947-1

Course Technology
20 Channel Center Street
Boston, MA 02210
USA

Cengage Learning is a leading provider of customized learning solutions with office locations around the globe, including Singapore, the United Kingdom,

Australia, Mexico, Brazil, and Japan. Locate your local office at: **international.cengage.com/region**

Cengage Learning products are represented in Canada by Nelson Education, Ltd.

For your lifelong learning solutions, visit **courseptr.com**

Visit our corporate website at **cengage.com**

Printed in the United States of America
1 2 3 4 5 6 7 12 11 10

To my students; their questions were a constant source of inspiration for this book.

Acknowledgments

I would like to thank Eric Kuehnl for all of his help and valuable input. Also, I would like to thank Andy Cook for his inspiration, vision, and support when I was starting with Digidesign.

Thanks to Mark Garvey and Kezia Endsley, for their seemingly never-ending patience and insight with me as we worked through this project.

In addition, I want to thank all of the Certified Pro Tools instructors and users I have met and developed friendships with over the years. You know who you are!

Last, but not least, I would like to thank Matt Donner for providing me with the opportunity to share my thoughts on this subject.

About the Author

Mark I. Altin is a freelance sound editor and composer along with being a teacher of Digital Audio Production in the Broadcast Electronic Media Arts Department at City College of San Francisco. Prior to this, he taught MIDI and digital audio at Full Sail University followed by working for Digidesign for over a half decade, developing its certified training program.

Contents

Chapter 2
Music Production Tips and Techniques　　　　　　　　　　　　　45

Chapter 3
Recording in Pro Tools   111

Chapter 4
Editing and Automation   157

Introduction

I started teaching Pro Tools back when the current version was 3.1, which ran on Pro Tools III hardware. Back then, it was only a TDM system, and it didn't do a whole lot other than record and sequence 16–48 mono tracks of audio. Looking back, my Pro Tools students had a blessing and a curse on their hands. It was a curse because the program severely limited their options in terms of what could be done with expressive editing. It was a blessing for much the same reason; its severely limited feature set meant there was less that needed to be learned.

Nowadays, as I see students take on the seemingly monumental task of learning how to use Pro Tools, I'm reminded of how much catching up students have to do. I don't envy the task, but I do respect the effort that students put forth in order to achieve success. In addition, I firmly believe that at the end of all that effort, Pro Tools users with a strong understanding of the software can create just about anything that they could sonically imagine.

As with spending time learning anything on your own, it is common to have some "gaps" in the understanding of how a system fundamentally works. This book is written to fill in many of the gaps that can occur when jumping in to Pro Tools, especially if you are starting with Pro Tools 8. It is my hope that these pages will clear up some of the confusing behaviors that Pro Tools seems to do at precisely the wrong times. Plus, it will provide you with some workflows that will speed up your productivity, and possibly give you a launching-off point toward developing your own relationship with this extraordinary audio production system.

This book isn't intended to be your sole source of everything Pro Tools. If you are looking for such a resource, I suggest using the Digidesign Training and Education program (see http://training.digidesign.com) for a complete look, from Post Production to Music Production to Audio Engineering. I had the great fortune to share in the development of that program, and I am very proud of the education it continues to inspire with its training partners.

How the Book Is Organized

Having taught Pro Tools for over a decade, I have read many books and taught many lessons on the subject. As such, I have found that there are two major ingredients required to assimilate the technical concept or technique into your existing repertoire. First, you need to have an experience in which to relate the concept or technique. This creates a context for the concept to take hold; it answers the always-present question, "Why am I learning this?"

Second, you need to understand the process for executing the technique. This process is usually laid out in a series of steps that outlines the process's basic execution; it answers the always-present question, "How do I do this?"

This book is designed to provide you with the "why" and the "how" in a single narrative format. There are many instances when I pull from my experiences as a Pro Tools user, as a teacher, and even as a witness to the many pitfalls that novice users experience, to provide context for the features described in this book. Given that everyone comes to Pro Tools with a slightly different set of experiences, you are also encouraged to answer the "why" question in your own way. In short, you will have a better chance of incorporating the concepts of this book if you know why they are important to you.

Answering the "how" is usually thought to be a simple matter of giving directions. I have mixed feelings on this subject. If the processes were outlined in a generic fashion, the book wouldn't be any more useful than what is available in the reference guide. However, if processes are too specific, there is the risk of not being able to work these processes into your own workflows. So, I opted for a hybrid.

Each tutorial is broken into a series of processes. In between each of the processes is an explanation as to why this process is important in the context of the tutorial. It's my hope that you not only find the tutorials enlightening, but that you are also able to extract individual processes to be used in your own workflows. In addition, by breaking down tutorials into processes, you'll never see super-long lists of steps. In general, I have tried to limit each of the processes to five or fewer steps, but there are a few exceptions when the process is a bit more lengthy.

This book is written in four chapters that are loosely based on the phases that music production Pro Tools users go through:

- Chapter 1, "Customizing Your Pro Tools Environment"—This chapter discusses the importance of customizing your work environment through the use of templates, window configurations, and memory locations.

- Chapter 2, "Music Production Tips and Techniques"—A large portion of this book is dedicated to this chapter. Within it, you will find many workflows for working with MIDI, Elastic Audio, tempo, virtual instruments, and more.

- Chapter 3, "Recording in Pro Tools"—This chapter illustrates some of the "off the beaten path" recording techniques you can use to create interesting effects or speed up production time. Also, there is an extensive section on setting up a system to use multiple drives and prevent errors.

- Chapter 4, "Editing and Automation"—This chapter covers many of the sound design features of Pro Tools. Within it, you will find compositing and editing techniques, exploring the real-time effects plug-ins included with Pro Tools 8, and some automation workflows.

Although you can use each chapter as an individual entity, it is probably best to run through Chapter 2 before Chapter 4, because Chapter 4 builds on the session that was created in Chapter 2. Chapters 1 and 3, however, are independent and can be tackled in whatever order is best for you.

The Target Audience

This book is targeted for hobbyists and professionals with some experience using the Pro Tools software. To get the most out of this book, it is advised that you have a basic understanding of the Pro Tools user interface.

Keyboard Shortcuts

There are no significant differences in the feature set between the Mac and Windows versions of Pro Tools. In fact, sessions created on one platform can be seamlessly transferred to the other without any conversion necessary. There is one difference that is pertinent to the readers of this book, however. Due to the fact that each platform has a unique set of modifier keys, keyboard shortcuts are slightly different between the Mac and Windows versions.

The book was written from the perspective of working on a Macintosh. The following modifier-key substitutions should be made if you are working on a Windows-based system.

- Replace use of the Command key in the text with the Control (Ctrl) key
- Replace use of the Option key in the text with the Alt key
- Replace use of the Control key in the text with the Start/Windows key

These substitutions will work for 90% of all keyboard shortcuts. For instance, the keyboard shortcut for the Undo command on Mac is Command+Z. Following the rules for substitution, the Windows shortcut is Ctrl+Z.

There are exceptions to this in cases where the OS overrides the application key commands. For example, pressing Option+Tab will move the edit cursor to the previous region boundary. If you were to follow the substitutions listed previously, you would press Alt+Tab, which happens to be the Windows key command to toggle between applications. In this case, the key command to move the edit cursor to the previous region boundary is Ctrl+Tab. In general, if these substitutions do not work, please refer to the keyboard shortcuts guide within the Pro Tools application by choosing Help > Keyboard Shortcuts.

System Requirements

This book was written to take advantage of the many components that are included with Pro Tools 8. I recommend that you have any version of Pro Tools 8 (HD, LE, or M-Powered), along with the Pro Tools Creative Collection. If you have any questions regarding your current system or whether you computer system is compatible with Pro Tools, please visit the Digidesign support website (http://www.digidesign.com/support) for the latest up-to-date compatibility information.

In addition to an available Pro Tools system, you will also need to copy the contents from the Audio Loops and Sounds DVD that is included with every shipping version of Pro Tools 8. If you updated to Pro Tools 8 via the website download, you may need to purchase a Replacement DVD set (which includes the Audio Loops and Sounds DVD) from the web store at http://shop.avid.com.

1 Customizing Your Pro Tools Environment

This chapter focuses on creating a perfect work environment so the Pro Tools interface won't be your stumbling block. In fact, with some practice of the concepts discussed here, it won't take long before Pro Tools becomes your ideal production assistant. You'll have everything exactly where you need it and can hide anything that creates clutter.

This chapter contains four tutorials that are designed to gradually build a complex template. They should be completed in order so you can see how each of the different Pro Tools customizations adds to the overall session template. Pro Tools is used in so many ways in the field, and it is therefore unlikely that every feature will find a home in your repertoire, at least not instantly. That is why I recommend that you pick one or two of the features and experiment with how they fit into your particular work environment after completing this chapter.

After all, reading and seeing a feature in action is easy; giving it a place in your workflow takes much more time. Stay with it, though; the results are worth it.

Tutorial 1: Taking Advantage of Templates

New to Pro Tools 8 are templates. Although the new version comes some standard templates, you will find that they will be most relevant after you create some of your own, custom ones.

Loading a Template

Templates are a great way to jump in and get started making music with Pro Tools, as many of the most common track setups and signal routing are already preconfigured. Before jumping in and creating your own template, it's a good idea to check out one (or a couple) of the templates that came with Pro Tools.

Opening the Songwriter-Singer template:

1. With Pro Tools already launched, choose File > New Session.

2. Click the Create Session from Template button.

3. Choose Songwriter from the pull-down menu.

4. Select Songwriter-Singer from the list, as shown in Figure 1.1.

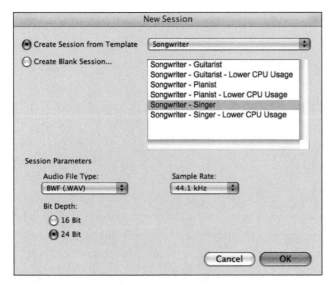

Figure 1.1 The New Session dialog box.

5. Click OK.

6. Pro Tools will ask you where you want to save the new session. For the purposes of this tutorial, you can choose to save it in your Documents folder. In the Save dialog box, navigate to your Documents folder and click Save.

The session should open, as shown in Figure 1.2. Some things to notice about this session are as follows:

- Some tracks are named.

- Comments are included for each track.

- There is no pre-roll set. Post-roll is set to 0|0|480 (which equates to one eighth note in Pro Tools).

- A timeline selection of 16 bars is already selected.

- Instrument tracks are configured with virtual instruments (not shown in the figure).

- The Drums track already has a drum beat sequenced in.

As you might have guessed, a number of considerations have been included in this session to help save time, but only if you work in a way that takes advantage of them. For instance, you may not like the drums that are sequenced on the Drums track, or you may want an Organ track instead of a MIDI Guitar track.

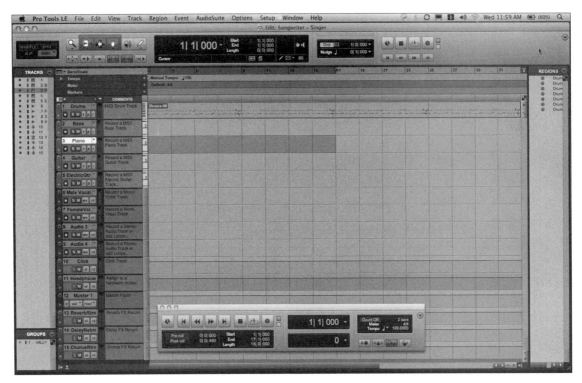

Figure 1.2 The Songwriter-Singer session template.

The point is that, although the included templates are a great start (and source of inspiration), there is no substitute for creating your own highly customized templates that address your particular needs and workflows.

The rest of this chapter focuses on creating a very specific type of template. The intention is to illustrate the degree to which templates can be customized. My hope is that you will take the concepts discussed here and make them your own to address your particular needs.

Creating a Template

First, you step through creating a music production template that will take advantage of some of the virtual instruments included with Pro Tools. At the start, this will be very similar to the template you just opened. However, you will see this template gain a high degree of sophistication as you build on it throughout the next three tutorials of this chapter.

Creating a Blank Session and Adding Some Tracks

This template is designed to allow a songwriter or composer to have instant access to a full suite of instrumentation (thanks to the many virtual instruments included with Pro Tools), plus be able to record vocals, acoustic guitar, electric guitar, and an analog synthesizer.

Creating a blank session and adding some tracks:

1. Press Command+N (Mac OS). Make sure the Create a Blank Session radio button is selected.

2. Press Shift+Command+N to bring up the New Tracks dialog box and create the following tracks, as shown in Figure 1.3:

Figure 1.3 The New Tracks dialog box.

> Four Mono Audio Tracks
>
> Two Stereo Audio Tracks
>
> Five Stereo Instrument Tracks
>
> Two Stereo Aux Inputs
>
> Two Stereo Master Faders

3. After the tracks are created, double-click the Track Name button on the first track to rename it.

> TIP: To quickly rename a bunch of tracks in Pro Tools, you can press Command+Right Arrow to jump to the next track. This will save you from having to press OK and then double-click on the next track.

4. For the purpose of this template, let's use the following names (based on the track order listed in Step 2):

    Vocal

    Vocal dbl

    Electric Guitar

Electric Guitar dbl

Acoustic Guitar

Acoustic Guitar dbl

Drums

Bass

Piano

Synth Lead

Synth Pad

Delay

Reverb

Master

Cue Master

Your Edit window should look like Figure 1.4.

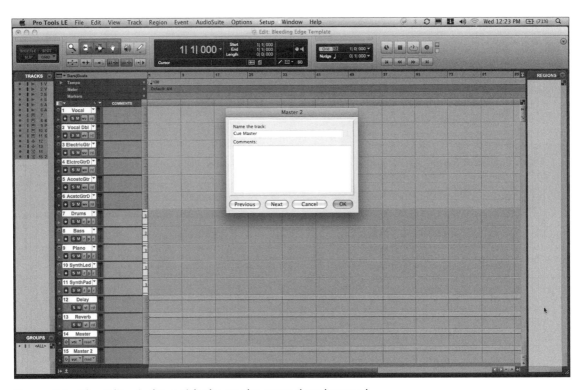

Figure 1.4   The Edit window with the tracks created and named.

Before continuing, it is important to note that, although the first Master track is set up correctly (it will adjust the level for outputs 1–2), you will need to assign the Cue Master to the proper outputs for it to function properly. In this particular studio, the headphone amp is connected to outputs 7–8 of the Digi 003 Pro Tools system.

Assigning the Cue Master to outputs 7–8:

1. Press Command+= (the equals sign) to bring up the Mix window.

2. On the Cue Master track, click on the output selector and choose Interface > Analog 7–8 (Stereo), as shown in Figure 1.5.

Figure 1.5 Select the Analog 7–8 (Stereo) outputs.

Now that you have a session and tracks in place, you need to add the virtual instruments and real-time delay and reverb effects. Both virtual instruments and real-time effects are treated as plug-ins to Pro Tools. As such, the process of setting them up is about the same.

Adding virtual instruments and real-time reverb and delay:

1. If it is not already shown, press Command+= (equals sign) to switch to the Mix window.

2. Display Inserts A–E (if they are not showing) by choosing View > Mix Window Views > Inserts A–E.

3. Click and hold the shaded area of Insert A (the topmost insert) for the Drums track and choose Multichannel plug-in > Instrument > Boom (Stereo). (Figure 1.6 shows the LE Insert menu.) (In Pro Tools HD, there is a TDM/RTAS submenu prior to the multichannel submenu.)

Figure 1.6   Select the Boom instrument plug-in on Insert A.

4. Repeat this step for the following tracks:

Bass: Vacuum

Piano: Mini Grand

Synth Lead: Vacuum

Synth Pad: Xpand2

Delay: Extra Long Delay II

Reverb: Air Reverb

Master: BF Essential Meter Bridge

Setting Up Presets

Now that you have the instruments and plug-in assigned (see Figure 1.7), it will be nice to have presets assigned to each of them. That way, you can just jump in and start creating music as soon as the session opens.

Figure 1.7 The Mix window with instruments and plug-ins assigned.

Setting up the presets for the virtual instruments and plug-in effects:

1. Click on the Boom plug-in to open the plug-in window.

2. In the Boom plug-in window, from the Librarian menu choose 068–085 > A Billion 076 (see Figure 1.8).

3. Repeat Steps 1 and 2 for the rest of the plug-ins. Here are the suggested presets for each:

    Bass Vacuum: 2 Bass > 17 Mean Mogue Bass

    Piano Mini Grand: 01 Real Piano

    Synth Lead Vacuum: 1 Leads > 21 Reso Rubber Lead

    Synth Pad Xpand2: 03 Huge Pads > +31 Oxygen Leak

Figure 1.8   Select a Boom preset from the plug-in's Librarian menu.

Delay Extra Long Delay II: Dly 8th note > 8th Dly Dotted [Long Delay]

Reverb Air Reverb: 02 Basic Medium

Of course, you can set the presets to be whatever you find most interesting, so feel free to change any of the presets if you want.

Adding EQ and Compression

While you are adding plug-ins, it might be a good idea to add EQ and compression for all of the tracks. If you are using a slower computer, however, you may want to avoid this step and just add them as needed.

Adding EQ and compression to all tracks in the session:

1.   While holding down the Option key, choose the 7-Band EQ 3 on Insert B of the Vocal track. You should notice that all of the stereo tracks now have a 7-Band EQ on Insert B. The Option key tells Pro Tools to add this plug-in to all mono tracks (see Figure 1.9).

Figure 1.9 EQ on all mono tracks.

2. Repeat Step 1. This time, however, add Compressor/Limiter Dyn 3 on Insert C (see Figure 1.10).

Now all mono tracks in your session have EQ and compression on them. Next, let's add them to the stereo tracks by repeating Steps 1 and 2 on the Acoustic Guitar track (don't forget to hold the Option key while you are making your assignments). Your Edit window should look like Figure 1.11.

Routing Sends

Just as with inserts, you can quickly assign all your track sends to feed the Delay and Reverb aux inputs.

Routing sends to Delay and Reverb tracks (and the Cue):

1. While holding down the Option key (Mac), on Send A of the Drums track, choose Buss > Buss 1–2. You should notice that all of the tracks now have Send A assigned to Buss 1–2.

Figure 1.10   The compressor is added to Insert B of the mono tracks.

Figure 1.11   EQ and compression are added to all tracks.

2.   Repeat Step 1. This time, assign Send F to Buss 3–4.

3.   One more time, repeat Step 1 on Send E, but this time, route it to Interface > Analog 7–8 (Stereo) (as shown in Figure 1.12).

Figure 1.12   Route Send E to Analog 7–8 (Stereo).

4.   Remove the sends from the Delay and Reverb tracks by clicking on the arrow next to the assignment and choosing No Send. This will prevent any chance of a feedback loop (see Figure 1.13).

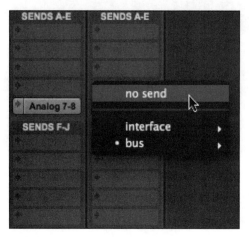

Figure 1.13   Remove sends from the Delay and Reverb tracks to avoid a feedback loop.

Now, you might be wondering why you chose Send F for reverb instead of B. Although both sends are identical on a technical level, there is a subtle but significant difference. Within each track, Pro Tools will allow you to see either all assignments in a given bank (A–E or F–J) or show a detailed view a single send (including a little fader, mute status, and pre/post status). Because the detailed send view can be set independently for each send bank, it is possible to show a detailed view of both Send A and Send F simultaneously.

Setting Up the Track Inputs

With Send 1 assigned to busses 1 and 2 and Send 2 assigned to busses 3 and 4, the next step is to configure the Delay and Reverb tracks to receive the audio sent over these busses.

Setting up the Delay and Reverb track inputs:

1.   On the Delay track in the Mix window, click on the input selector.

2.   Choose Buss > Buss 1–2 (shown in Figure 1.14).

Figure 1.14 Set the input of the Delay track to Buss 1–2 (Stereo).

3.   Repeat the process on the Reverb track, but choose Buss > Buss 3–4.

Now, when you raise the level of any send, a copy of the audio signal will be routed through either the Delay track (by raising Send A) or the Reverb track (by raising Send F)—or through both (by raising both sends).

Saving the Session as a Template

You are just about done with your template. All that remains is to arrange the windows in the way you want to see them when the template opens, and to save this session as a template.

Saving this session as a template:

1. Choose File > Save As Template.

2. Click on the Install Template in System radio button.

3. Choose Add Category from the Category pull-down menu, as shown in Figure 1.15.

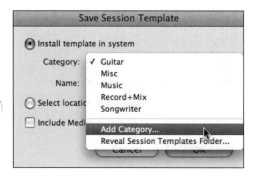

Figure 1.15 Choose Add Category from the Category pull-down menu.

4. In the New Category section, type "My Studio Templates" and click OK, as shown in Figure 1.16.

Figure 1.16 Name the category.

5. In the Name section, type "Sketchpad (Basic w/EQ and Dyn)," as shown in Figure 1.17.

6. Click OK to save the template.

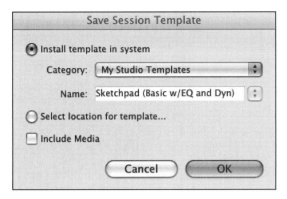

Figure 1.17   Give the template a descriptive name.

At this point, you have a basic template that contains a full complement of virtual instruments, all with EQ and compression, with quick access to delay and reverb. Although this template is sufficient for a general workflow, there are many more customizations that can be done. By taking advantage of custom I/O setups, Window Configurations, and Memory Locations, you can have a highly customized template that supports your particular workflow.

Tutorial 2: Customizing the I/O Setup

As your sessions become more complex, you may start to feel a little frustration in trying to remember what is routed where and which busses are used for a particular task. Patching and routing logs have been part of the studio workflow for a long time. Such logs were, in fact, commonplace back in the days before Pro Tools. With that said, if you are actually keeping a log, you may find this tutorial to be a great time saver.

The I/O Setup window is an interface where Pro Tools relates the ins and outs of the hardware and software to logical names. By default, these names are chosen based on the particular hardware and the software. Although all of the inputs, outputs, and busses are aptly named, they are a bit generic. The true power of this window comes to bear when you group and rename them to fit your specific studio and/or session. These custom names eliminate (or drastically reduce) the need to keep a log.

In the tutorial that follows, you will be renaming the inputs, outputs, and busses that were used in the previous tutorial's template. Because there are numerous inputs and outputs of the hardware that can be used with Pro Tools, this tutorial assumes that you're using a Digi 002.

Renaming the Standard Outputs

First, you will rename the outputs that are in use. In this scenario:

- Outputs 1 and 2 feed the monitor speakers.

- Outputs 3 and 4 feed the headphone amp.

- All other outputs aren't being used.

Renaming the outputs:

1.   Choose Setup > I/O, as shown in Figure 1.18.

Figure 1.18   The I/O menu option from the Setup menu.

2.   Click the Outputs tab.

3.   Rename Outputs 1–2 "Monitor."

4.   Click the disclosure triangle to reveal that the sub-paths have already been renamed "Monitor.L" and "Monitor.R" (see Figure 1.19).

5.   Rename the path Output 3–4 "Phones."

6.   Uncheck the checkboxes for the other output paths to deactivate them (if you need them in the future, they only need to be rechecked in this dialog box).

7.   Your outputs should look like Figure 1.20. If they do, click OK.

Now is a good time to see how changes to the I/O setup relate to your session. You may have already noticed that your Mix window looks a little different. You should now see "Monitor" instead of what was previously written in the output selector. If you click on the output selector, you will also notice that you have Phones as your only other choice under the Interface sub-menu. Through editing the I/O setup, you have created logical names and streamlined the choices to reflect only the options that are actually connected, as shown in Figure 1.21.

Renaming the Standard Inputs

Now let's apply this type of optimization to the inputs. Many project studios (and professional studios, for that matter) have certain pieces of equipment that are always connected to specific

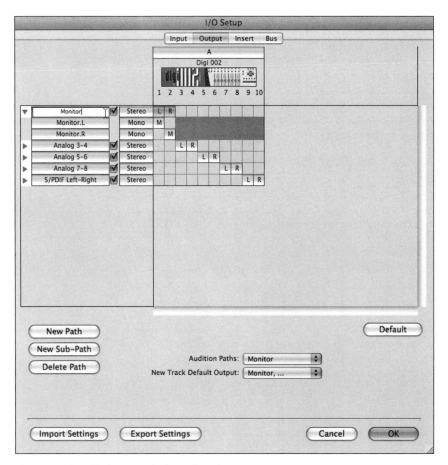

Figure 1.19   I/O Setup window showing outputs.

inputs. This prevents breaks in the creative flow, as everything is already connected and ready to go. Pro Tools can take advantage of that consistency by renaming the generic Input 1 to be the name of the device that is connected to it!

For this section, this tutorial is going to assume that the following equipment is connected to the first four inputs of the Digi 002:

- A matched pair of TLM 170 mics is plugged into Inputs 1 and 2.

- A Les Paul guitar is plugged into Input 3.

- A Moog Voyager is plugged into Input 4.

The microphones may be used either as a stereo pair or individually, so it is fine if they are linked in a stereo path. The sub-paths, however, will also need to be renamed in order to remove the .L and .R that Pro Tools automatically assigns to the sub-paths when a path is renamed.

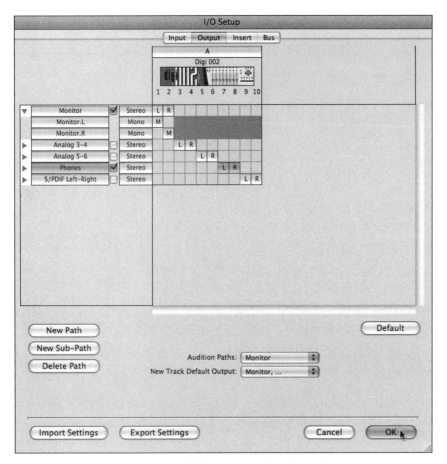

Figure 1.20 Your outputs should be renamed as shown here.

Renaming Input 1–2 paths and sub-paths:

1. Choose Setup > I/O to open the I/O Setup dialog box.

2. Click the Inputs tab.

3. Double-click on the first path to rename it.

4. Type "TLM 170 1–2."

5. Click the disclosure triangle to reveal the sub-paths.

6. Delete 1-2.L and replace it with a 1. Press Return.

7. Delete 1-2.R and replace it with a 2. Press Return.

Both the Les Paul and Moog Voyager are going to be used only as mono sources. As a result, you don't want to have them linked in a stereo path. Since Pro Tools links odd-even numbered

These outputs used to
read "Output 1-2"

This output used
to read "Output 7-8"

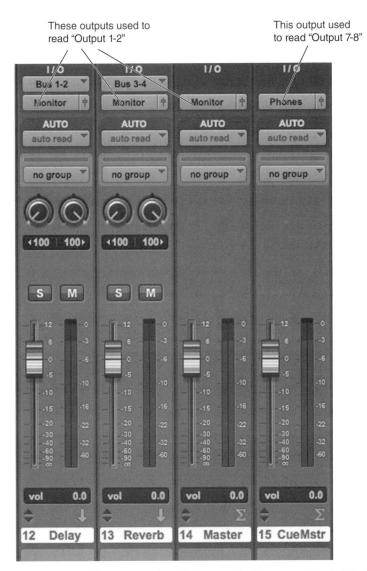

Figure 1.21   Changes to the I/O Setup window are reflected in the Mix and Edit windows.

inputs into stereo paths by default, you will first need to delete the stereo path for Input 3–4 before creating two mono paths.

Deleting input path Input 3–4 and creating two mono paths:

1. With the I/O Setup dialog box still open and showing the Inputs tab, click on the path Input 3–4.

2. Click the Delete Path button in the lower-left corner of the I/O Setup dialog box, as shown in Figure 1.22 (or press the Delete key).

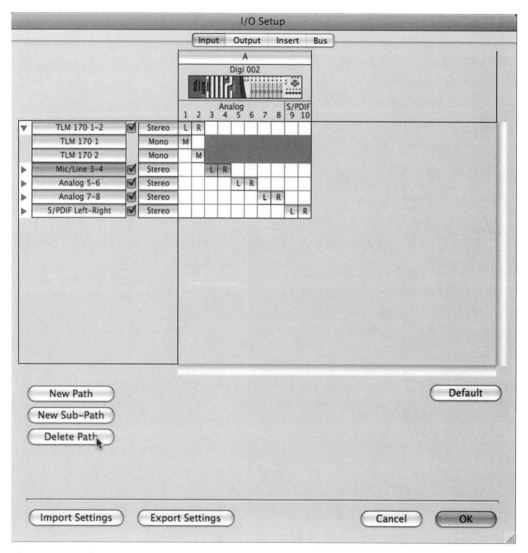

Figure 1.22 The I/O Setup window showing inputs.

3. Click on the New Path button twice to create two new paths (or press Command+Shift+N).

4. Rename Path 1 "Les Paul."

5. Press the Tab key to move to the next path.

6. Rename Path 2 "Voyager."

7. Set the Les Paul path to Mono and click on the Analog Input 3 column, as shown in Figure 1.23.

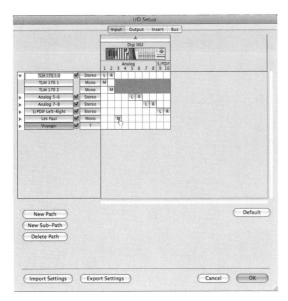

Figure 1.23   Make sure there is an M in the Analog Input 3 for the Les Paul path.

8.   Set the Voyager path to Mono and click on the Input 4 column.

9.   Click and drag both the Les Paul and Voyager paths up so they are under the TLM 1–2 path.

Your inputs should be set up like Figure 1.24. While you have the window open, go ahead and rename the busses that are currently in use. This means that Buss 1–2 and Buss 3–4 will be renamed "Delay" and "Reverb," respectively. It is a probably not a good idea to delete the busses that aren't currently being used. As a template, there is a good chance that they will be used during a session, and it is always quicker to activate an existing path than create one from scratch.

Renaming the Busses

Use these steps to rename the busses that are in use:

1.   With the I/O Setup dialog box still open, click on the Buss tab.

2.   Double-click to rename Buss 1–2 "Delay."

3.   Double-click to rename Buss 3–4 "Reverb."

4.   If your I/O Setup dialog box looks like Figure 1.25, click OK.

As seen in Figure 1.26, there is no longer a need to remember where your equipment is connected because Pro Tools now shows the names of your equipment as the routing options. With

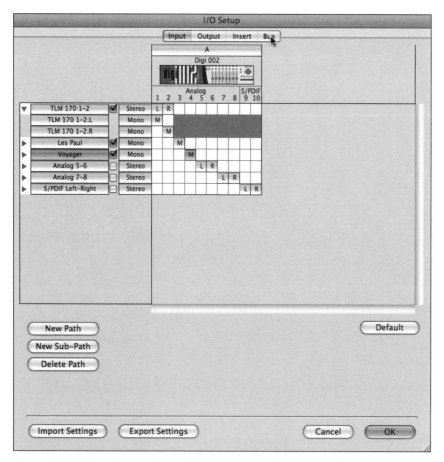

Figure 1.24 Your inputs should be assigned and renamed like this.

your I/O setup customized to the specifics of how your studio is set up, you will find that routing audio through your session will be more efficient, and there will be less of a chance that a routing error will occur.

Tutorial 3: Setting Up Window Configurations

Window Configurations are a great way to quickly jump between multiple arrangements of windows. Although this may seem trivial at first, you might be surprised by the amount of time you can spend just moving windows around in order to complete a simple task. If you find that you constantly have to rearrange your windows between two or more layouts, setting up Window Configurations will be a huge benefit. Furthermore, Window Configurations can be assigned to Memory Locations (covered in the next tutorial) for an even more customized work environment!

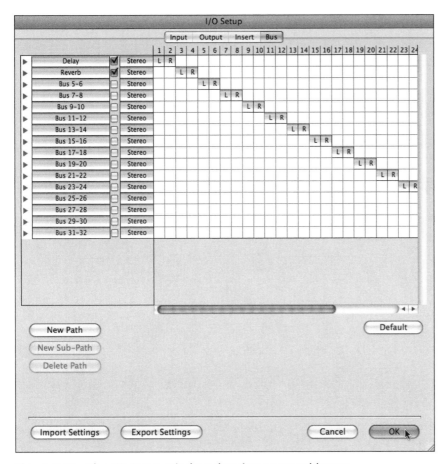

Figure 1.25   The I/O Setup window showing renamed busses.

Figure 1.26   The renamed paths now appear in the Track Input Selector pop-up menus.

For the purposes of the Sketchpad template, you will create a few Window Configurations that will keep your creativity flowing. Before jumping in, it is worth noting that Window Configurations are highly dependant on your computer monitor setup and resolution. So you may want to have your monitor (or monitors, if you use more than one) arranged and set to the resolution that is comfortable to work with.

Creating a Reset Window Configuration

It is always smart to start with a Reset Window Configuration. That way, you can always jump back to the same starting point.

Creating a Reset Window Configuration:

1. Arrange the Edit, Transport, and Mix windows, as shown in Figure 1.27.

Figure 1.27 Arrange your Mix, Edit, and Transport windows as shown here.

2. Choose Window > Configurations > New Configuration to open the New Window Configuration dialog box (or press decimal and then the + key on the numeric keypad).

3. Make sure the topmost radio button, called Window Layout, is selected.

4. Name the Window Configuration "Reset" (see Figure 1.28).

5. Click OK.

Creating a MIDI Editing Window Configuration

Now, you can create a layout that shows an Edit window with the MIDI Edit pane and inserts shown.

Creating a MIDI Editing Window Configuration:

1. Show only the instrument tracks.

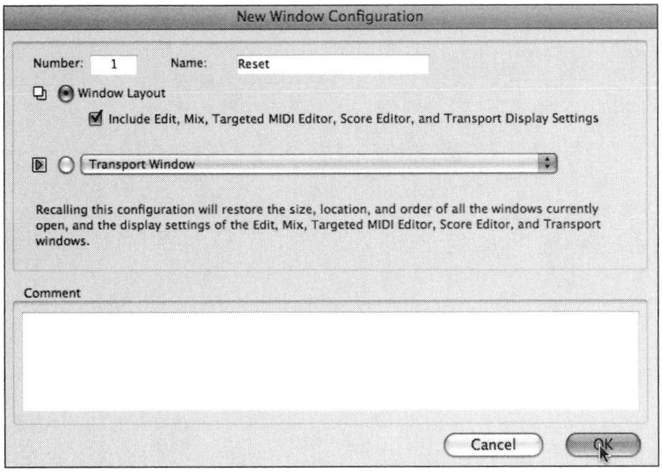

Figure 1.28 Name your first Window Configuration "Reset."

2. Make sure that only the following are showing in the Edit window:

Inserts A–E

Instrument

Real-time MIDI properties

3. Show the MIDI Editor pane by choosing View > Other Displays > MIDI Editor. The Edit window should look similar to Figure 1.29.

4. Choose Window > Configuration > New Configuration (or press decimal then the + key on the numeric keypad). Again, this will open the New Window Configuration dialog box.

5. Name the Window Configuration "MIDI Editing."

6. Choose the Window Layout radio button.

7. Make sure that the Include Edit, Mix… checkbox is checked.

8. Click OK.

Some musicians like to edit MIDI in a score format. Fortunately, Pro Tools 8 has a separate editor (called the Score Editor) that can display the score in a separate window. (The Score Editor can also be displayed in the MIDI Edit pane of the Edit window.) Not only is the Score Editor a great place to edit and arrange the MIDI data, but it also can be used to lay out and preview the score before printing—a handy feature if you plan on providing notation to the members of your band. As such, here is an opportunity to move beyond the Edit window and allow the Score Editor to be center stage. It is also a smart idea to include the Mix and Transport windows. This way, you can handle quick adjustments to levels and tempo in a cinch.

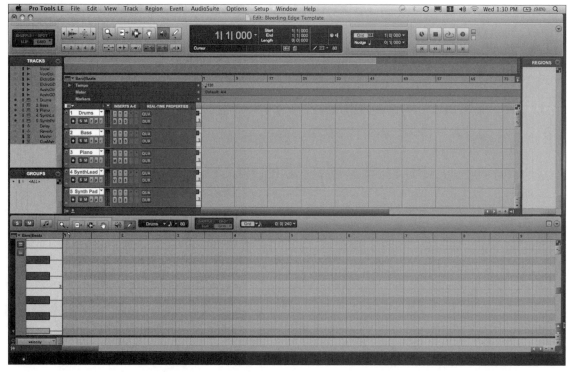

Figure 1.29   The Edit window with the MIDI Edit pane.

Creating a Score Editor Window Configuration

Creating a Score Editor Window Configuration:

1. Close the Edit window and open the Score Editor, Mix window, and Transport window by selecting them from the Window menu.

2. Arrange the windows as shown in Figure 1.30.

3. Choose Window > Configurations > New Configuration.

4. Choose the Window Layout radio button.

5. Make sure that the Include Edit, Mix… checkbox is checked.

6. Name the configuration "Score Editing."

7. Click OK.

Creating a Vocal Detail Window Configuration

The next configuration focuses on everything related to the lead vocals. Because singers/song-writers tend to take special care with the vocal track, it will really speed up their workflow by

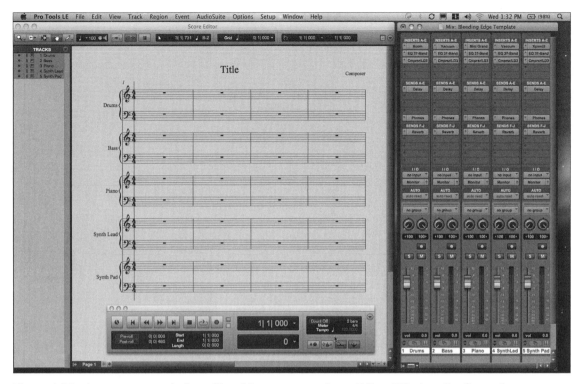

Figure 1.30 Arrange your windows like this to create a Score Editor Window Configuration.

having all of their settings instantly appear before them on the screen! Of course, you can extend this idea to all of the major instruments in the template, but this tutorial focuses only on the vocals.

One final note before creating this configuration—the Window Configuration feature doesn't have any way to specifically choose which tracks are displayed in the Edit window. As such, this Window Configuration will be used in the Memory Locations tutorial later in this chapter to ensure that the vocal track always appears.

Creating a Vocal Detail Window Configuration:

1. Open the Edit and Mix windows and hide the Tracks and Regions lists. Arrange these windows as shown in Figure 1.31.

2. Shift+click on the Vocal Track EQ plug-in to open and un-target it. This will allow you to have multiple plug-in windows open simultaneously.

3. Shift+click the Vocal Track Compressor plug-in to open and un-target it.

4. Arrange the windows as shown in Figure 1.32.

5. Create a new Window Configuration. Name this Window Configuration "Vocal Detail."

Figure 1.31 The Edit and Mix windows, arranged for this example.

Creating a Mixing Window Configuration

Now, let's put together a mixing configuration. You will also include a "targeted" plug-in window (so any plug-in will open in the same place) and an "un-targeted" plug-in master meter (so that it won't disappear, regardless of which plug-in gets clicked on). Finally, you will include a send window (for a more detailed view of a send) and a Memory Locations window (which will make it a snap to jump between different marker Memory Locations).

Creating a Mixing Window Configuration:

1. Show the Mix window and close the Edit window (if it is showing).

2. Open the BF Essential Meter Bridge on the Master track and un-target it (or simply use Shift+Click).

3. Click on any 7-band EQ in the Mix window to open a second plug-in window.

4. Click on any send to open a send pop-up window.

5. Press Command+1 on the numeric keypad to show the Transport window.

6. Press Command+5 on the numeric keypad to show the Memory Locations window.

7. Arrange the windows as shown in Figure 1.33.

8. Save the Window Configuration and name it "Mixing."

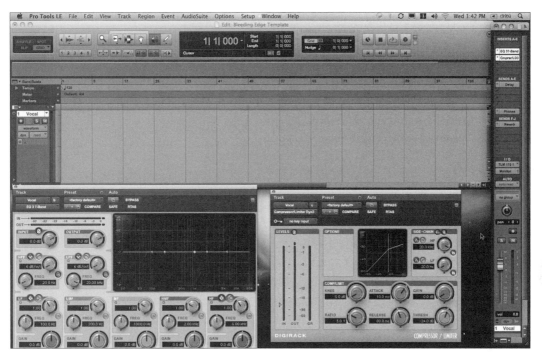

Figure 1.32 Vocal Detail window arrangement.

Figure 1.33 The Mixing window arrangement.

Creating Edit Views Window Configurations

The next two configurations are for the various views of the Edit window. There are times when you're working in Pro Tools and you find that you need to access a setting in the Edit window. Although Pro Tools is good at allowing users to show and hide many of the different views, it can be disruptive to constantly mouse around to show a pane, only to have to put it away. With Window Configurations, however, you can show all of the settings with a click of your mouse and then hide them again just as quickly.

Create a Show All Edit window view:

1. Choose View > Edit Window Views > All, as shown in Figure 1.34.

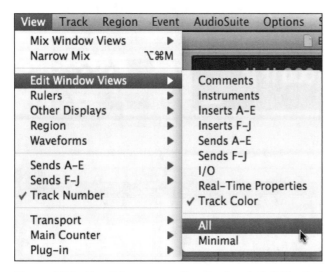

Figure 1.34 Use this menu option to show all Edit window views.

2. Display the Track Show/Hide and the Region lists. The Edit window should look like Figure 1.35.

3. Choose Window > Configurations > New Configuration.

4. Click the Edit Window Only radio button.

5. Name this Window Configuration "Edit Show All" (see Figure 1.36).

6. Click OK.

Now you should create a configuration that hides all of the views, thus providing you with a much larger work area.

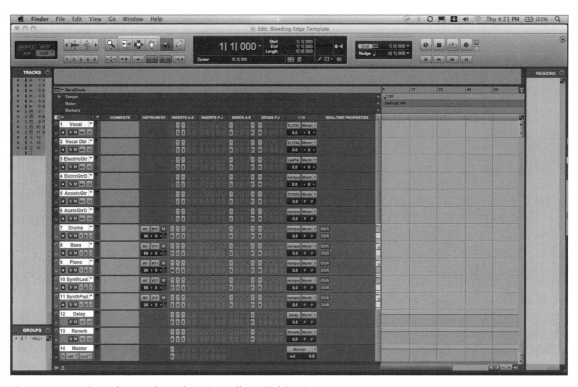

Figure 1.35   The Edit window showing all available views.

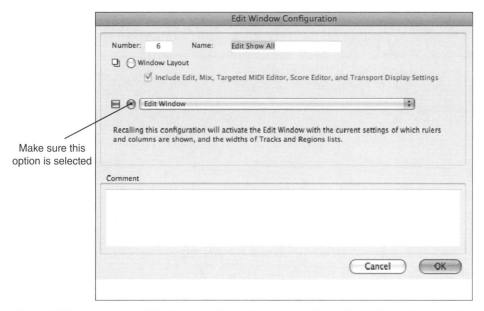

Figure 1.36   Creating a Window Configuration that adjusts the Edit window to show all views.

Creating a Hide All Edit Windows view:

1.   Choose View > Edit Window Views > Minimal.

2.   Hide the Track Show/Hide and Region lists. Your Edit window should look like
     Figure 1.37.

Figure 1.37   The Edit window showing minimal views.

3.   Choose Window > Configurations > New Configuration.

4.   Click the Edit Window Only radio button.

5.   Name this Window Configuration "Edit Minimal." (See Figure 1.38.)

6.   Click OK.

These last two configurations only involve the Edit window, which means they are much less
invasive than the others. By recalling either of these configurations, you will only manipulate the
Edit window. This means that any MIDI editors, Score Editors, plug-in windows, and so on will
not move or be affected in any way.

All in all, this is really just the start of how you can use Window Configurations. Pro Tools can
store up to 99 Window Configurations, so feel free to create more of your own!

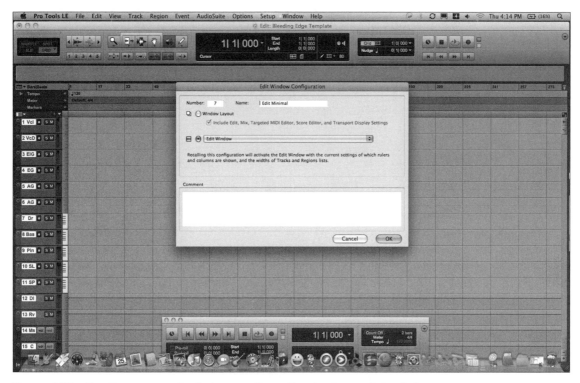

Figure 1.38   Creating a second window configuration to show minimal views.

Recalling Your Window Configurations

Now that you created a few Window Configurations, you're ready to put them to use! The following are a few ways to recall Window Configurations. Although using the numeric keypad might feel awkward at first, it is truly the fastest way to move from one configuration to another.

You can recall Window Configurations using one of the following methods:

- On the numeric keypad, press decimal (.), followed by the Window Configuration's number, and then asterisk (*).

- Choose Window > Configurations > (select the desired Window Configuration from the submenu).

- Click on the Window Configuration in the Window Configuration list.

Updating Your Window Configurations

Lastly, you may find that after working with a particular Window Configuration for a time that it could be tweaked a bit. Fortunately, there is an easy way to update your Window Configuration so the old one is replaced with a new one. For this tutorial's purpose, you can update the Reset Window Configuration to hide the Tracks list.

Update the Reset Window Configuration to hide the Tracks list:

1. Recall the Reset Window Configuration.

2. Hide the Tracks list.

3. Choose Window > Configurations > Update "Reset" (see Figure 1.39).

Figure 1.39 Updating a Window Configuration is easy.

That's it! Now every time you recall the Reset Window Configuration, the Edit window will hide the Tracks list.

Tutorial 4: Using Memory Locations to Customize Your Pro Tools Environment

Although Window Configurations focus on the size and placement of windows (and some additional view settings like Edit window and Mix window views), they don't store many other settings that will be very useful in sessions. Fortunately, this is where Memory Locations come into play.

Many people will often use the terms "Memory Locations" and "markers" interchangeably. The fact is that they are quite different. *Markers* are one of many things that can be stored in

Memory Locations. Although you will see Memory Locations used in many different ways throughout this book, the focus of this tutorial is to use Memory Locations to quickly adjust what is being shown in the Edit and Mix windows. Window Configurations created in the previous tutorial will also be linked with the Memory Location so the placement and size of windows can be recalled with all of the other attributes.

Organizing Memory Locations Storing a Memory Location is next to effortless with Pro Tools. When you want to store something in a Memory Location, you simply have to press the Enter key on your numeric keypad (not the Return key on your main keyboard). When Enter is pressed, Pro Tools will open a dialog box for the next available Memory Location. You just need to choose which attributes you want to store and press Enter again to lock them in. Although this works very well for laying down markers in real-time, it can present some other challenges when using Memory Locations for other tasks.

Pro Tools has the ability to store up to 999 Memory Locations for each session. If you just continue to let Pro Tools store each Memory Location sequentially, it can be quite a challenge to keep track of which Memory Location is storing which attributes. Fortunately, there are a few ways to organize your Memory Locations! The first step, however, is to come up with a plan for how you want to access them.

Many Pro Tools users find that they like to have the first 49 or so Memory Locations open for markers in their project. As a result, for this tutorial, you will start entering "non-marker" Memory Locations at 50. Since there are nearly infinite ways to incorporate the different properties of Memory Locations, you may find that your organizational system goes beyond merely "starting at 50." For instance, Memory Locations 50–59 could be zoom settings, 60–61 could be track show/hide settings, and 70–71 could be group enables. The possibilities are seemingly endless, but the results in refining your workflow with Memory Locations will most certainly be worth the effort.

In general, when creating functional Memory Locations, some of the things to keep in mind are:

- Which tracks are being viewed and what size they should be set to

- What is the appropriate zoom level for the timeline

- What is the appropriate Window Configuration (see previous tutorial)

- What are the most appropriate pre-roll and post-roll settings

Creating a Reset Memory Location

As with Window Configurations, it is a good idea for the first Memory Location you create to be a reset location. Also, unless you specifically know that you don't want an attribute to be reset, it is always good to store a value for each of the general properties.

This particular reset is going to:

- Show all tracks on-screen at once

- Zoom out to show an overview of the timeline

- Recall the Reset Window Configuration

- Set pre/post-roll to zero

Creating a Reset Memory Location:

1. Show all tracks.

2. Recall the Reset Window Configuration.

3. Adjust the height of all the tracks so they are visible within the window.

4. Click on Zoom Preset 1 to set the zoom level.

5. Make sure the pre-roll and post-roll are set to zero in the Transport window. Your screen should look like Figure 1.40.

Figure 1.40   Your session should look like this.

6. Press . (decimal)+50+Enter on the numeric keypad to open the New Memory Location dialog box.

7. Select None in Time Properties area, check all the general properties, and choose 1: Reset in the Window Configuration pop-up menu, as shown in Figure 1.41.

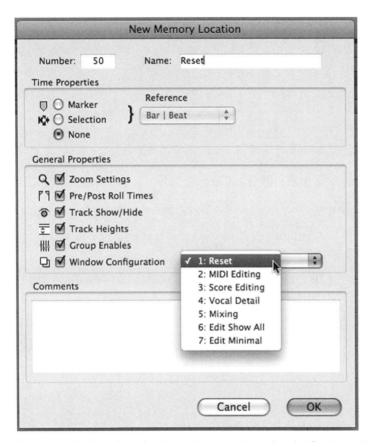

Figure 1.41   Creating the Reset Memory Location in the New Memory Location dialog box.

8. Name the Memory Location "Reset."

9. Click OK.

Notice how you included all of the general properties in the Reset Memory Location? This was done to ensure that Pro Tools will reset all properties regardless of what gets modified in the future. If you find that there is a property that you don't want to have reset, you can update the Memory Location to not include that property. Editing and updating Memory Locations are covered later in this tutorial.

Creating a MIDI Production/Editing Memory Location

With the Reset Memory Location created, the next Memory Location will be useful during a MIDI production session. In this Memory Location, there will be separate zoom setting for the docked MIDI Editor.

This Memory Location will:

- Show only instrument tracks

- Zoom in to show about 16 measures of music in the Edit window and four measures in the docked MIDI Editor

- Recall the MIDI Edit Window Configuration

- Set a 2-beat pre-roll

Creating a MIDI Production and Editing Memory Location:

1. Show only the instrument tracks in the Edit window.

2. Recall the MIDI Editing Window Configuration that you created in a previous tutorial.

3. Click on Zoom Preset 2 (or press Command+2 on the keyboard, not the numeric keypad) to set the zoom level.

4. Click on the + and – next to the MIDI Edit pane scroll bar (as shown in Figure 1.42) to show roughly four bars in the MIDI Edit pane.

Figure 1.42   These + and – buttons in the bottom-right corner adjust the zoom level for the MIDI Edit pane in the Edit window.

5. Set the pre-roll and post-roll to 0|2|000.

6. Press Command+K to turn off pre-roll and post-roll.

7. Press . (decimal)+51+Enter on the numeric keypad to open the New Memory Location dialog box.

8. Select None in the Time Properties area, check all the general properties, and choose 2: MIDI Editing in the Window Configuration pop-up menu, as shown in Figure 1.43.

9. Name the Memory Location "MIDI Production and Editing" and then click OK.

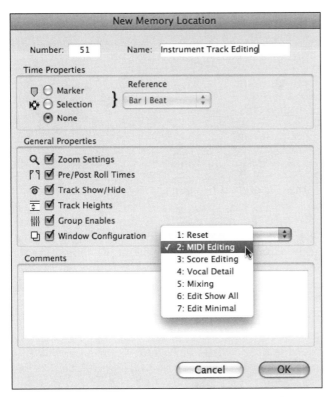

Figure 1.43 Creating the MIDI Production and Editing Memory Location in the New Memory Location dialog box.

Creating a Vocal Recording/Editing Memory Location

Next, you can make a Memory Location that takes advantage of the Vocal Detail Window Configuration. As stated earlier, the Window Configurations generally focus on window placement, not track show/hide or track height. As such, depending on which other tracks are showing, recalling the Vocal Detail Window Configuration will have unpredictable results in the Edit window.

By adding the Vocal Detail Window Configuration to a Memory Location, not only can you recall the window layout, but you can also hide any unnecessary tracks and adjust the track height.

This Memory Location will:

■ Show only the vocal track

■ Zoom in to show about 16 measures of music in the Edit window

■ Recall the Vocal Detail Window Configuration

■ Set a 2-bar pre/post-roll

Creating a vocal recording/editing Memory Location:

1. Hide all tracks except for the vocal track and set its Track Height to Large.

2. Recall the Vocal Detail Window Configuration.

3. Set the pre-roll and post-roll times to two bars (2|0|000).

4. Press Command+K to turn off the pre/post-roll.

5. Adjust the Zoom to show about 16 measures on the timeline.

6. Press . (decimal)+52+Enter on the numeric keypad to open the New Memory Location dialog box.

7. Select None in the Time Properties area, check all the general properties, and choose 4: Vocal Detail in the Window Configuration pop-up menu, as shown in Figure 1.44.

8. Name the Memory Location "Vocal Track Editing" and then click OK.

Figure 1.44 Creating the Vocal Track Editing Memory Location with a Window Configuration.

Setting and Disabling Pre/Post-Roll You may be wondering what is the point of setting the pre/post-roll times, since you subsequently press Command+K to disable them. Although it is a matter of personal preference, many people prefer to have pre/post-roll off by default. With that said, however, it can be a great timesaver to have the pre/post-roll set to usable values. That way, when you need pre- or post-roll, you just have to press Command+K. As a bonus, Pro Tools allows you to store custom pre- and post-roll times within the Memory Location. Since the Memory Locations that you are making for this template are based on configuring the work environment of a given task, it makes sense to have the pre- and post-rolls set to appropriate times.

By having a workable pre/post-roll time already set, you just need to press Command+K to enable pre/post-roll. In the case of this template, you will have two beats for MIDI editing and two bars for vocal recording/editing.

Creating a Mix Window Memory Location

The last Memory Location will be for mixing. Just as before with the Vocal Detail Window Configuration, while recalling the Mixing Window Configuration brings up the windows in the correct layout, it doesn't show all of the tracks. As such, you will have to create a Memory Location for your Mixing Window Configuration in order to ensure that all the tracks will be shown.

This Memory Location will:

- Show all tracks in the Mix window

- Recall the Mixing Window Configuration

- Set a 2-bar pre-roll

(There is no Edit window or timeline display, so zoom settings are irrelevant.)

Creating a Memory Location for your Mixing Window Configuration:

1. Show all tracks, except for the Cue Master track.

2. Recall the Mixing Window Configuration.

3. Make sure that the pre-roll and post-roll times are still set to 2|0|000. If they aren't, set them now.

4. Press . (decimal)+53+Enter on the numeric keypad to open the New Memory Location dialog box.

5. Select None in the Time Properties area, check all the general properties, and choose 5: Mixing in the Window Configuration pop-up menu.

6. Name the Memory Location "Mixing." See Figure 1.45.

7. Click OK.

Figure 1.45   The Mixing Memory Location with Window Configuration.

Recalling a Memory Location

Now that you have Memory Locations, you should practice recalling them.

You can recall Memory Locations 50–53 using one of the following methods:

■   On the numeric keypad, press decimal (.) followed by Memory Location number and then the decimal (.) again.

■   Press Command+5 (on the numeric keypad) to display the Memory Location list, and then click on the desired Memory Location.

Editing a Memory Location

At this point, you have created Memory Locations in a very general fashion. This is to ensure that they will work with a wide variety of sessions that may come from this template. As you work on projects, however, you will most likely find that you need to edit some Memory Locations to suit the specific needs of the current session. For the purposes of this tutorial, you will edit the MIDI Production Memory Location (which should be location 51) to include the Master fader.

Editing a Memory Location:

1. Recall location 51.

2. Show the Master track.

3. While holding Option, choose Track Height > Fit to Window from the Track Options pop-up menu of any track.

4. Press Command+5 to open the Memory Locations window.

5. In the Memory Locations window, choose Edit "Instrument Track Editing" from the pop-up menu, as shown in Figure 1.46.

6. Click OK in the New Memory Location dialog box.

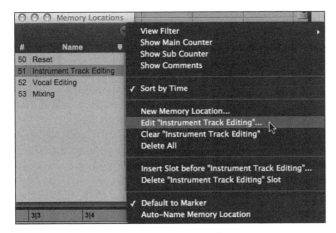

Figure 1.46   Editing a Memory Location.

The result is that the Memory Location is updated to include the new track.

Summary

In this chapter, you have seen how the use of templates, customized I/O setups, Window Configurations, and Memory Locations can create a flexible work environment for the creative singer/songwriter. Although this template may work well for this particular purpose, it is really only the beginning. Pro Tools is used in many different scenarios, and you should use the concepts covered in this chapter to create a customized environment for your own specific scenarios.

As a result, crafting a quality template is as much an art form as the projects that take advantage of them. Hopefully, the previous four tutorials will serve merely as a starting point as you find new ways to streamline the repetitive tasks that you encounter in your day-to-day work with Pro Tools.

2 Music Production Tips and Techniques

In recent years, Pro Tools has seen an inordinate amount of upgrades to its music production toolset. Furthermore, Pro Tools 8 represents the most complete music production toolset available.

Rather than trying to cover the entire music production feature set in one long list, this chapter aims to provide you with a few select features that you will most likely benefit from. In addition, you will find more in-depth explanations and experiments designed to better aid you in understanding what Pro Tools is doing behind the scenes. The hope is that with this understanding, you will be empowered to find even more uses for the techniques described here.

Lastly, the point of this chapter (and this book as a whole) is to provide you with ideas to help improve your efficiency with the software. So, although all of the content in this chapter might not be flashy or take advantage of the latest whiz-bang features, it will improve your production speed.

TIP: The tutorials contained in this chapter assume that you have copied the entire contents of the Pro Tools Audio Loops and Sounds DVD (which ships with Pro Tools) directly to your hard drive, as this will help make searching for sound files easier. If you do not have this DVD, feel free to substitute any loops mentioned with ones from your own library.

Tutorial 5: Using Skeleton Tracks to Create Song Structure

A *skeleton* region is a region that has no auditory significance but aides in organizing and getting around your session. The term is not something that is officially designated in the software; it is mostly a term created by a community of editors who work with them (they have to call them something, right?).

In this tutorial, you use skeleton regions to organize your session. Although it may be hard to understand their importance here at the start, through this chapter, you will see some ways that skeleton regions can speed up some common workflows.

The Importance of Session Organization

Many of you may scoff at the idea of structuring the timeline, due the perception that it will reign in your creativity or stifle your ideas in some way. Although freeform impromptu recording can be inspiring and provide you with a treasure trove of ideas, in the end those ideas will need to be organized in some fashion. Whether you preemptively decide on the session structure or not is entirely up to you. The main point is that once you decide on a structure, illustrating it within the Pro Tools session will allow you to work much faster than you may initially realize.

Why Not Just Use Markers and Selection Memory Locations?

Of course, it's perfectly valid to use markers and selections stored in memory locations. In fact, many people do use markers to lay out song structure. Down the production road, however, they usually find that these fall short in a couple of areas.

For one, you only have a single Marker Ruler in your session. This ruler can get quite cluttered when marking ins and outs that overlap. Figure 2.1, for instance, shows the relatively common occurrence whereby a vocal melody has a pickup into the next bar. This can be confusing to look at, making it more difficult to follow the song structure, and defeats the whole purpose of putting the markers in there in the first place. Because you use more than one track to illustrate song structure, you can quickly and clearly show the layout of the vocal tracks and backing tracks.

Figure 2.1   Markers can be confusing when you're trying to show a complex song structure.

Figure 2.2 shows the same example as described previously, except with skeleton regions.

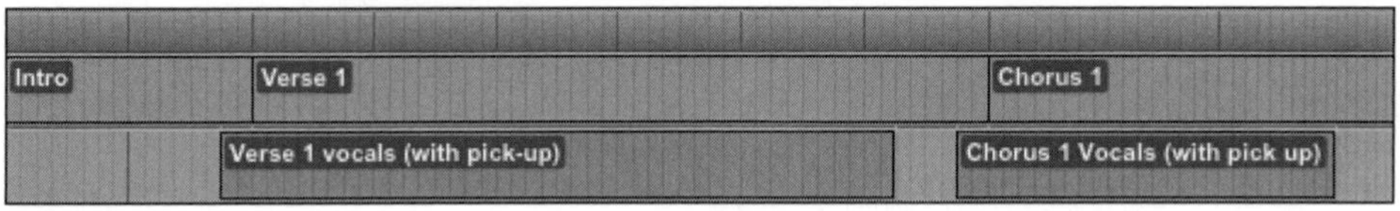

Figure 2.2   Using multiple skeleton tracks allows you to clearly organize a complex song structure.

Another issue is that selection-type memory locations do not show up in the Marker Ruler. This means that you don't have any graphic illustration of song form whatsoever. Furthermore, if you don't meticulously label the selection memory locations, you might find it difficult to find the proper one. With a skeleton region, however, making a selection is as easy as clicking the region with the Grabber.

Lastly, by using skeleton tracks to illustrate your session structure, you free up the Marker Ruler for other information (such as song lyrics or timeline notes, discussed later).

Creating Skeleton Regions

An easy way to lay out the flow of a new project is to use blank MIDI regions. Although the MIDI regions won't contain any data, they will provide you with a graphical layout. Here is a quick and dirty list of just a few benefits that can be derived from mapping out your track with skeleton regions:

- **Session has a definite end time:** The end of the last ghost region is the end time. This is great for features that take advantage of "session end time" (the Option+Return key command, double-clicking the Zoom tool, and when you loop a region to the end of the session, to name three). Also, this will give you a very tight estimate of the overall duration of the project.

- **Visual layout of the song structure:** You can influence the focal point(s) of the song. Knowing where the "huge climatic crescendo" of the song is will certainly help you build the song for the biggest possible impact. Plus, with the structure laid out, you will see how much work is left to do, which is important if you are on a deadline.

- **Selecting and arranging parts of your session are a breeze:** You can quickly double the chorus or slow down the tempo of the bridge by simply clicking on the ghost region and extending the selection to the relevant tracks and rulers. This is covered in more detail throughout the chapter.

Of course this is just a quick list; as you work with skeleton regions, you are sure to find new ways to work them into your workflow. Let's put this into practice by creating a simple song form.

Organizing your project with skeleton regions:

1. Create a new session (for clarity and the specific nature of the content in this tutorial, it is better to start with a blank session rather than the template created in Chapter 1).

2. Create a new MIDI track, drag it to the top of the Edit window, and name it "Form."

3. Put Pro Tools in Grid mode and set your grid value to one bar.

4. Select the first two measures of the session.

5. Press Option+Shift+3 on the keyboard to consolidate the empty selection into a region (shown in Figure 2.3).

6. Double-click the region in the Regions list and rename it "Intro."

7. Repeat these steps for each of the other sections in your song. Figure 2.4 shows the following sections:

    Intro (2 bars)

    Section A (6 bars)

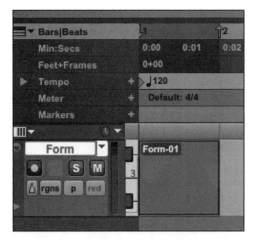

Figure 2.3 Using Consolidate to create an empty MIDI region.

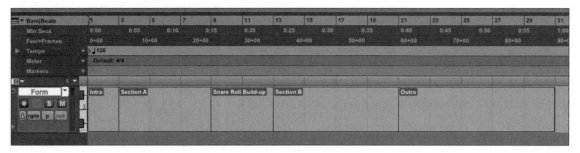

Figure 2.4 Complete skeleton track with regions.

Snare Roll Build-Up (4 bars)

Section B (8 bars)

Outro (10 bars)

If needed, you can repeat the process to create a second skeleton track if you have a complex song layout with overlapping sections. This tutorial, however, will move forward with only one.

Adding Lyrics and Notes with Markers

Now that the skeleton tracks are taking care of illustrating the song form, markers can be used to add lyrics, cue notes, or any other information that you may want to indicate on the timeline. By taking advantage for the Comments Section of memory locations, you can have a set of lyrics or other notes stored in your session. It's always a good idea to have the lyrics handy if you are working with artists or songwriters (they can be touchy if you misquote one of their lyrics in conversation).

In addition to adding lyrics, markers can also serve as repositories for timeline comments, either for your own notes or for purposes of collaboration. In this tutorial song, there aren't any lyrics, but there are a number of "hit" points that you should make note of.

Adding markers to contain song timeline notes:

1.   Set the insertion cursor to 9|1|000.

2.   Press the Enter key in the numeric keypad to open the Edit Memory Location dialog box.

3.   Choose Marker in the Time Properties Section.

4.   Type "Drum Roll Starts" in the Name field.

5.   Type "Use 1/16 note snare from Boom" in the Comments field.

6.   If your Edit Memory Location dialog box looks like Figure 2.5, click OK.

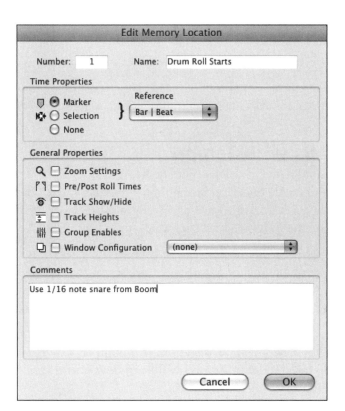

Figure 2.5   Completed Edit Memory Location dialog box.

Repeat these steps to add markers with the following comments:

Bar|Beat Location	Name	Comment
13|1|000	Drum Roll Ends	Add a drum and bass loop
21|1|000	Drum Breakdown	One-bar drum breakdown

With the Marker Ruler showing, you can hover over a marker to see the comments (shown in Figure 2.6) or read the lyrics.

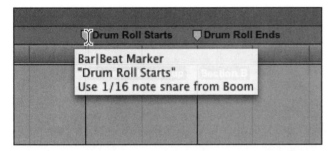

Figure 2.6   Marker comments are shown when you hover over a marker in the Edit window.

And that wraps up this tutorial. Although there is no actual sound, the initial conception of your song is laid out on a timeline. All that is left to do is decide on an initial tempo and fill in all of the silence with cool-sounding stuff.

Tutorial 6: Becoming Friends with Tempo

Pro Tools' approach has a unique way of handling tempo. This could be because at its inception the primary focus of Pro Tools was on audio engineering (replacing multi-track tape machines and editors), not on music composition. As a result there wasn't a strong need to work with tempo, other than creating a tempo map for the purposes of a click track to aid musicians.

Today, Pro Tools is used as a much bigger part of the music-creation process. As a result, Pro Tools has been steadily increasing its music production/composition feature set since Pro Tools 5. With Pro Tools 8, just about every major feature that you could need for music production is available, and this includes an extensive set of tempo tools.

Due to the extensiveness of these tools, this chapter covers tempo in two separate tutorials. In this tutorial, you learn how to set the initial tempo by manually entering a number, as well as basing it on the recorded tempo of an audio loop. In addition, you will learn how to conform a sound file to match the tempo of the session.

In Tutorial 9 (later in this chapter), you will add dynamic tempo changes to your session and recalculate the average tempo so the music fits a specific duration.

Setting an Initial Tempo

By default, Pro Tools assigns each new session to a default value of 120 BPM by creating a tempo marker in the Tempo Ruler and enabling the Conductor Track button in the Transport window. If you want a song to play slower or faster, you need to change this initial tempo. There are two ways you can do this:

- Disable the Tempo Ruler by clicking on the Conductor Track button in the Transport window and setting the tempo manually.

- Leave the Tempo Ruler enabled and just edit the initial tempo marker.

Disabling the Tempo Ruler is a quick and easy way to set and adjust the tempo. The main downside, however, is that Pro Tools will be unable to respond to any dynamic tempo changes in the session. This isn't much of a problem, though, if you are just sketching out a song with a single tempo or producing a song with no tempo changes.

Disabling the Tempo Ruler and manually setting the tempo:

1. Show the Transport window.

2. Display the MIDI controls if they aren't already showing.

3. Click on the Conductor Track button so that it is no longer blue (shown in Figure 2.7).

Figure 2.7   The Conductor Track Enable button in the Transport window.

4. Click in the Tempo display of the Transport window, and either type a value of the desired tempo or tap the T key on your keyboard at the desired tempo (shown in Figure 2.8).

5. Press Enter to lock in the tempo.

Figure 2.8   Entering the tempo in the Transport window.

If you plan on having some tempo changes throughout the song (which is the case if you are following along with this tutorial), you need to have the Conductor Track button active. So, it is better to edit the initial tempo marker in the Tempo Ruler. If you disabled the Conductor Track button, enable it now.

Editing the initial tempo marker to set the session tempo:

1. Press Return to go to the start of your session.

2. With the Tempo Ruler showing, double-click on the initial tempo marker (see Figure 2.9) to open the Tempo Change dialog box.

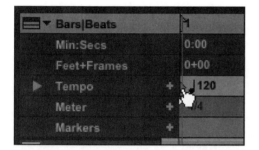

Figure 2.9 Double-click on the initial tempo marker to open the Tempo Change dialog box.

3. In the Tempo value field, either type the desired value or tap the T key at the desired tempo (see Figure 2.10).

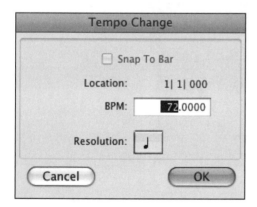

Figure 2.10 The Tempo Change dialog box.

That was easy enough, but what if you have an audio loop that you want to build the song around? It would be nice to import the audio loop and have Pro Tools determine its tempo. Lucky for you, Pro Tools can do that by taking advantage of a function called Identify Beat. Read on to find out how!

Basing the Session's Tempo on an Audio Loop (Using Indentify Beat)

In the last section, you learned of ways to set the session's tempo by manually entering (or tapping) it into the Transport window or by editing the initial tempo marker. Next, you will set your attention on making Pro Tools calculate the session tempo based on an audio loop.

In order for Pro Tools to calculate the tempo accurately, you need to have a true loop or be able to select one bar of *audio*, not the grid (remember, the Pro Tools grid will not be accurate until it has identified the tempo of the audio). In other words, Pro Tools should loop on a region or selection, and there should be no audible glitches or stutters when it jumps from the end point back to the start.

In addition to the loop being true, you will need to tell Identify Beat the musical duration of the loop in bars | beats | ticks. If this data is entered incorrectly, you might not get the results you were hoping for.

Fortunately, Pro Tools 8 ships with a large number for pre-made loops. Before using Indentify Beat on your own recording, it is a good idea to practice on these loops for a couple of reasons:

- They are already cut to be perfect 1-, 2-, or 4-bar loops.

- Most of these loops already have the tempo contained in the name. This will serve as a check to see if you were able to correctly identify the tempo of the loop.

Let's start by importing one of these loops into your session.

Importing an audio loop into a session from the Workspace:

1.   Press Option+; (semicolon) to open the Workspace.

2.   Click the Find button (see Figure 2.11).

3.   Enter "084 Hip Hop 808 Kick" into the Filename field.

4.   Drag the audio file from the Workspace to the Tracks list (see Figure 2.12).

Pro Tools will automatically create a new track and name it the same name as the file. On occasion, you may see a dialog box asking if you want to import the tempo of the audio file. This is because Pro Tools analyzed the file's tempo at one point in the past. This is a convenient feature that allows you to keep in the creative flow. It can also be useful to understand how Identify Beat is used to set the session tempo. So, for the purposes of this tutorial, choose No.

Using Identify Beat to calculate the tempo of the audio file:

1.   Click on the loop region with the Grabber tool to select it.

2.   Choose Event > Identify Beat.

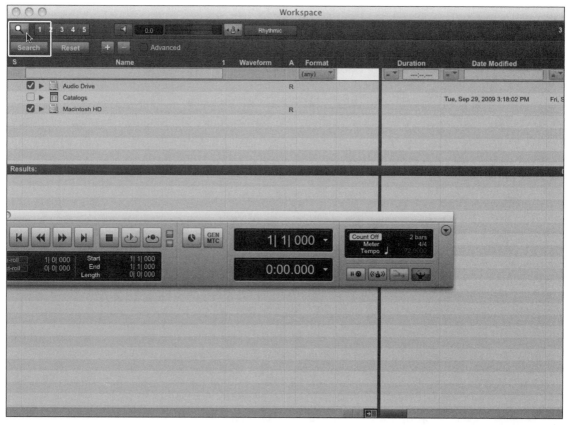

Figure 2.11 The Find button in the Workspace.

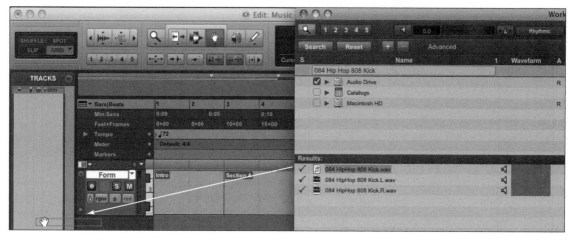

Figure 2.12 Dragging an audio file from the Workspace to the Tracks list.

3. In the Add Bar/Beat Markers dialog box, set the start time to 1 | 1 | 000 and the end time to 3 | 1 | 000 (see Figure 2.13).

4. Click OK.

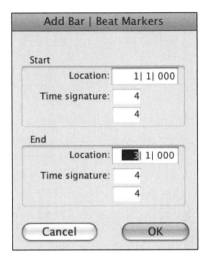

Figure 2.13   The Add Bar | Beat Markers dialog box.

Pro Tools will calculate the tempo and conform the grid based on the length of the selection (in samples) and the tick value that you entered in the Add Bar | Beat Markers dialog box. This is done when Pro Tools automatically inserts the tempo events in the Tempo Ruler.

Conforming Audio to a Session's Tempo

With the initial tempo set, the next challenge is to incorporate other loops of different tempos into the session. Since Identify Beat adjusts the session tempo to fit the audio loop, it can't be used here. Instead, you need to find a way to adjust the actual tempo of the audio loop to match the session. Fortunately, Pro Tools' TCE Trim tool makes conforming audio to your session's tempo super easy.

Using the TCE Trim Tool to Conform Tempo

The Time Compression/Expansion (TCE) Trim tool is an easy way to conform audio to a new tempo. Essentially, if you import a true loop at a tempo other than the session tempo, the loop will be too short or too long to fit on the grid perfectly. Figure 2.14 shows 2-bar audio loops on two tracks. The recorded tempo on the top track is slower than the session tempo. As a result, it looks like it is longer than two bars on the grid. Conversely, the bottom track contains a loop recorded at a faster tempo, so it looks like it is less than two bars.

With the TCE Trim tool, the top loop can be time compressed, and the bottom loop can be expanded (or stretched) so they both can precisely fill two bars in the session. Figure 2.15

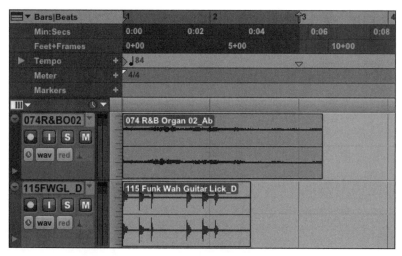

Figure 2.14   These loops don't match the session tempo.

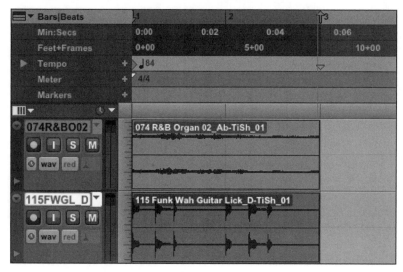

Figure 2.15   After using the TCE Trim tool, both loops now match the session tempo.

shows the same loops after the TCE Trim was applied, which you do by dragging the end for the region to the appropriate length. Once the mouse is released, Pro Tools will do all of the recalculations needed in order to make the audio fit the new timeframe. The effect on the audio is that the slower (longer) loop will now play back faster than it was originally recorded, and the faster (shorter) loop will play back slower than it was recorded; thus both will match the session tempo. Now it is time for you to give it a try.

To enhance the hip-hop kick drum, let's add some Latin jazz drums.

Importing 088 Latin Jazz Drums into your session:

1.   In the Workspace, search for 088 Latin Jazz Drums.

2.   Drag the file from the Workspace to the Tracks list. This will create a track, name it the same as the file, and place the region on the track at the session start.

The session is 84 BPM, but the Latin Jazz Drums file is 88 BPM. Just like the example that was provided previously, the 1-bar loop of the Jazz Drums doesn't quite fill up one bar on the grid (see Figure 2.16).

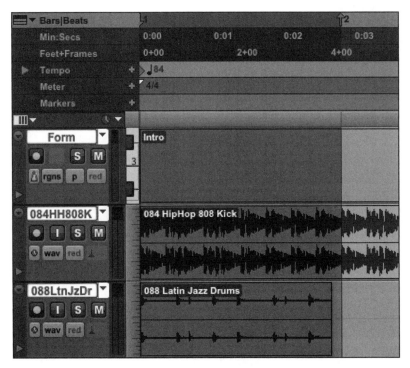

Figure 2.16   The Latin Jazz Drums loop suffers the same problem; it does not match the session tempo.

Again, just like the previous example, using the TCE Trim, you can stretch the Jazz Drum loop to fill the extra time. Due to the fact that the music usually sub-divides the bar equally, by stretching the loop to fit the bar, you are actually slowing the tempo by precisely the required amount. Since there is no need to calculate or convert speed percentages to BPM, this is a very fast and convenient way to adjust tempo.

Stretching 088 Latin Jazz Drums to match the session tempo:

1.   Place Pro Tools in Grid Edit mode by clicking on the Grid button in the upper-left corner of the Edit window.

2.   Click and hold the Trim tool in the Edit window, and then choose the TCE Trim tool (shown in Figure 2.17).

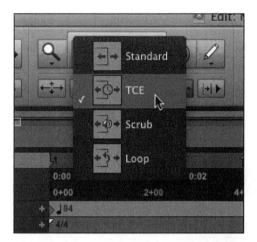

Figure 2.17   The TCE Trim tool is found in a pop-up menu in the Tools Section of the Edit window.

3.   Drag the end of the 088 Latin Jazz Drums loop to bar 2 (shown in Figure 2.18).

Figure 2.18   Stretching the loop with the TCE Trim tool.

After a brief calculation, the resulting version of the loop is perfectly in time with the session! Let's take a quick moment to look at the filename. Notice that the name of the file has changed from 088 Latin Jazz Drums to 088 Latin Jazz Drums-TiSh_01. This is because when Pro Tools stretched the audio file, it actually created a completely new file on your hard disk. The "TiSh" abbreviation stands for *time shift*. Pro Tools will automatically add an abbreviation that matches the type of TCE process that is used. Since this new file was customized for your session (and is no longer 88 BPM), you may want to rename it to be more accurate.

Renaming the region and disk file for the modified 088 Latin Jazz Drums loop:

1.   With the Grabber tool, double-click on the region.

2.   In the Name dialog box, rename the file "084 MP Latin Jazz Drums" (see Figure 2.19).

3.   Click the Name Region and Disk File radio button to select it.

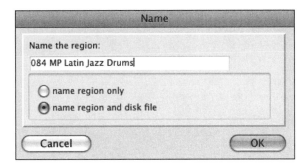

Figure 2.19   The Name dialog box is used for renaming a whole region.

Introducing Elastic Audio

With version 7.4, Pro Tools added Elastic Audio to its feature set. As the name indicates, this feature allows you to stretch your audio in various ways. Elastic Audio is a very powerful feature that will be discussed in more detail in Chapter 4. In this chapter, you will focus on using Elastic Audio to align the tempo of an audio file to your session. Now, you may be scratching your head and thinking, "Well, isn't that what I just did using the TCE Trim tool?" You wouldn't be wrong for wondering about their differences. In fact, the TCE Trim tool changes its behavior slightly when Elastic Audio is enabled. You will learn more about their differences in a little bit. For now, however, let's perform a little experiment before enabling Elastic Audio properly.

As stated in the previous section, when you use the TCE Trim tool (without Elastic Audio), it will render a completely new file at the desired length and tempo. If you were to use the TCE Trim tool again on the same file, it will process the rendered file to the new length. Each time you TCE a rendered file, you add artifacts to the sound quality. You can hear this by simply taking the loop you adjusted in the previous section and TCE trimming it some more.

Trimming the 084 MP Latin Jazz Drums to one beat, and then back to one bar:

1. Set the Grid to 0|1|000 by clicking on the Grid pop-up menu and choosing ¼ Note (shown in Figure 2.20).

2. With the TCE Trim tool, drag the loop end to 1|2|000 (shown in Figure 2.21).

3. Now, drag the loop end back to 2|1|000 (shown in Figure 2.22).

4. Repeat Steps 2 and 3 twice more.

If you are zoomed in on your monitor, you may already notice that the waveform looks a bit different. When you time-compressed the file, Pro Tools had to select and remove a bunch of sample data from the audio recording in order to fit the relatively large region into such a small space. In fact, because one beat is a quarter of a bar, Pro Tools had to remove three out of every four samples to make the region fit. Then, when you stretched it out, Pro Tools had to calculate the new length by adding samples back in. Because it had to add three samples for every one

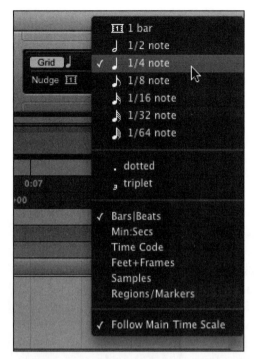

Figure 2.20 Choose ¼ Note in the Grid pop-up menu.

Figure 2.21 Compressing the loop to one beat (one ¼ note).

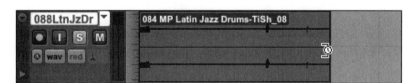

Figure 2.22 Stretching the loop back to one bar.

sample in the recording, it had to perform a lot of guesswork in order to fill in all of the time. When you play the loop, you can hear the artifacts of all that guesswork. Of course, you may love the sound that it creates, but if you were hoping to get the same sound you started with, you are out of luck.

For comparison purposes, let's keep this distorted loop and place a fresh version of this loop on a new track. You may want to rename this loop (and the track that the loop is on) 084 MP Distorted Drums in order to prevent any confusion.

Drag 084 MP Latin Jazz Drums from the Regions list to the Tracks list. As you may have noticed, each time the TCE Trim tool is used, it creates a new audio file on your disk. This means that you can always get back to the original version by dragging it out from the Regions list (shown in Figure 2.23).

Next, let's enable Elastic Audio and try the same experiment.

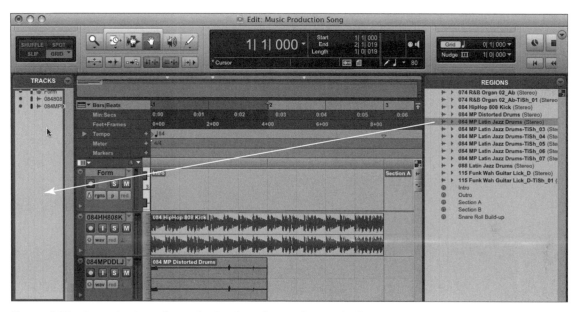

Figure 2.23 Drag the loop from the Regions list to the Tracks list.

Enabling Elastic Audio

Elastic Audio is enabled on a track-by-track basis. To enable it, you need to click on the Elastic Audio Plug-in selector (shown in Figure 2.24).

Figure 2.24 Elastic Audio Plug-in selector.

Enabling Elastic Audio on the newly created track:

1.   On the newly created track (it should be called 084 MP Latin Jazz Drums), click on the Elastic Audio Plug-in selector.

2.   Choose Rhythmic from the pop-up list (shown in Figure 2.25).

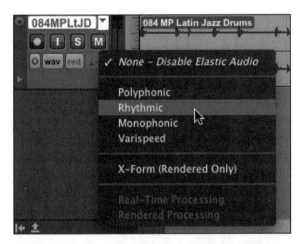

Figure 2.25   The Rhythmic Elastic Audio plug-in is well suited for most percussive loops.

The waveform will briefly go gray as Pro Tools analyzes the audio. Once analysis is complete, the waveform will return to its previous color, and Elastic Audio will be enabled. Also, a little emblem in the upper-right corner of the region indicates that the region is currently elastic. Now it is time to try the same experiment.

Trim the new 084 MP Latin Jazz Drums to ¼ Note and then back to one bar. If you solo the track and play it back, you will notice that the compressing and expanding of the region didn't cause any artifacts this time. This is because when Elastic Audio is enabled, Pro Tools will always do the calculations from the original audio analysis. Since you have effectively returned the audio back to its original state, Pro Tools didn't need to do any calculations. It just needed to recall the original waveform. Another difference in having Elastic Audio enabled is that Pro Tools doesn't render a new file each time the TCE Trim tool is used.

The last difference is that Elastic Audio can function in real-time. This means that when it is used in conjunction with the Ticks timebase (discussed in the next tutorial), it will automatically conform the audio regions to any dynamic tempo changes.

If you have a fast computer, you might want to have Pro Tools automatically enable Elastic Audio every time you create a new track.

Making Pro Tools enable Elastic Audio when it creates a new audio track:

1.   Choose Setup > Preferences.

2. From the Processing tab, choose the Enable Elastic Audio on New Tracks checkbox (shown in Figure 2.26).

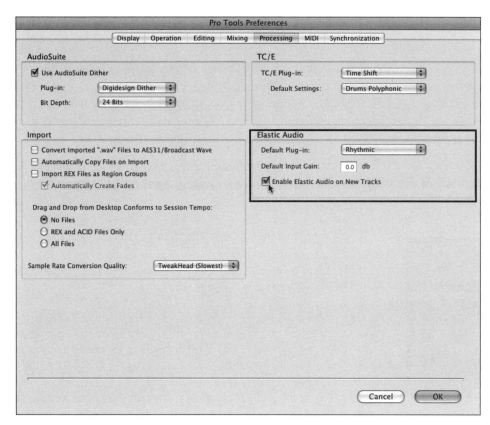

Figure 2.26   Elastic Audio Preferences from the Processing tab.

You also have the option of choosing the default real-time plug-in and input gain. Polyphonic seems to be the most flexible, and unless you have very specific needs, there isn't much of a reason to change it here (you can always change the plug-in on the track if you find you aren't happy with the results on a specific audio file).

Potential Downsides to Elastic Audio

With all the benefits regarding Elastic Audio, the question that begs to be asked is "Why not just have Elastic Audio enabled on all tracks, all the time?" Although there is no one stopping you from working that way, there are a couple of points to be aware of before you do so.

First, even though Elastic Audio will always refer to the original audio file, it can still create artifacts. That is one reason that there are four real-time modes (Polyphonic, Rhythmic, Mono-phonic, and Varispeed). Each mode processes the audio in a slightly different way and has a slightly different array of controls. In the end, time compression and expansion is as much an art as it is a science. Although the preference described previously will get you started in the right direction, it won't entirely replace the need to tweak some of the more advanced controls, which mitigates some of the convenience of having it automatically enabled in the first place.

Second, due to Elastic Audio being a real-time process, your computer can take a significant performance hit. In many cases, it is a good idea to keep Elastic Audio off until you are ready to add some tempo changes. Then, once all the tempo changes are complete, disable Elastic Audio (by clicking on the Elastic Audio Plug-in Selector and choosing None). Pro Tools will ask if you want to revert to the original or commit the warped audio regions before disabling Elastic Audio. If you are happy with the way the tempo changes sound, clicking Commit will render new audio files, thus freeing up processing power (further optimizations are discussed in Tutorial 10).

If you find that you need to have Elastic Audio enabled on all of your tracks, but your computer can't keep up with all of the real-time processing, you can enable Rendered Processing mode (shown in Figure 2.27).

Figure 2.27 Enabling Rendered Processing mode.

In Rendered Processing mode, the computer will take all warped regions offline (gray waveform) for the moment in order to process the file before putting it online again. This should ease the burden on your computer, but you will have to suffer with less than instant results each time you change the tempo.

Previewing and Importing Loops with Elastic Audio

By taking advantage of the Workspace, you have the option to preview loops at the session tempo, regardless of the file's original tempo. In addition, it is also possible to have Pro Tools automatically conform the audio to the session tempo. This can be convenient when you want to quickly build up a rhythm section comprised of files recorded at different tempos (as long as all of the loops are true).

To illustrate this in practice, let's add to the loops that are already in the session, while taking advantage of tempo conform preview along with listening to the existing tracks.

Using tempo conformed preview in the Workspace to quickly add to the Rhythm Section:

1.   With Loop Playback enabled, select the Hip Hop kick loop and start playback.

2.   In the Workspace, click on the Conform to Session Tempo button shown in Figure 2.28.

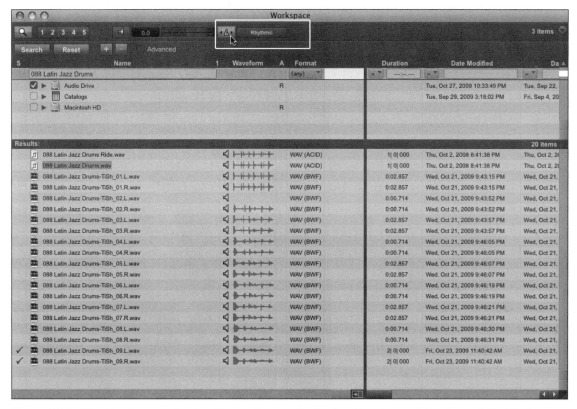

Figure 2.28   The Conform to Session Tempo button in the Preview Controls Section of the Workspace.

3.   Use the search commands in the Workspace to find a Pro Tools loop of your liking.

4.   Click on one of the search results and press the spacebar. The loop will begin to play at the next down beat. This will ensure that you will hear it in tempo and in context with the other loops playing.

5.   When you find a loop that suites you, drag it to the Tracks list. The loop 080 Indian Basstabla 02 was used.

A new track should have been created, Elastic Audio has already been enabled, and the loop should automatically be conformed to the session tempo.

TIP: It is possible to have Pro Tools automatically analyze audio files for Elastic Audio by selecting Audio Files Conform to Session Tempo from the Workspace's Browser menu.

Special Considerations Regarding REX Files

The workflows illustrated in the previous section work equally well for any supported format. If you have a REX file library, however, there are a couple more options available to you.

REX files are somewhat unique because they typically contain slice, tempo, and length metadata. For all intents and purposes, this metadata is similar to the analysis data that Pro Tools creates for use with Elastic Audio. In some of the higher-end REX libraries, the producer tweaks this metadata to give you the best possible results. As such, Pro Tools can use the metadata as seamlessly as it analyzes a wave file.

Pre-Analyzed Elastic Audio

Pro Tools can use the REX file metadata as the analysis from Elastic Audio with 100% confidence. What this means for you is that Pro Tools can import REX files and take advantage of Elastic Audio without needing to take the time to re-analyze them. Working with REX files in this way is the default workflow, but if you are finding it not to be the case, you can check and adjust the preferences.

Setting Pro Tools to import REX files as Elastic Audio:

1.   Choose Setup > Preferences.

2.   On the Processing tab, make sure Import REX Files as Region Groups is unchecked (see Figure 2.29).

Slicing and Grouping

In addition to working with REX files as Elastic Audio, Pro Tools can import the REX file, slice it into little regions based on the metadata, and then group the regions into a single region group. This will replicate the standard REX file functionality seen in most programs and sampler workstations. If the REX file is on a ticks-based track, the individual regions will stay locked to their assigned positions in the bar. Slowing the tempo down significantly will cause gaps to appear in between each of the regions (although the region group will appear as one long region; see Figure 2.30).

Speeding up the tempo significantly will cause the regions to overlap (shown in Figure 2.31).

Setting Pro Tools to import REX files as region groups:

1.   Choose Setup > Preferences.

2.   In the Processing tab, make sure Import REX Files as Region Groups is checked.

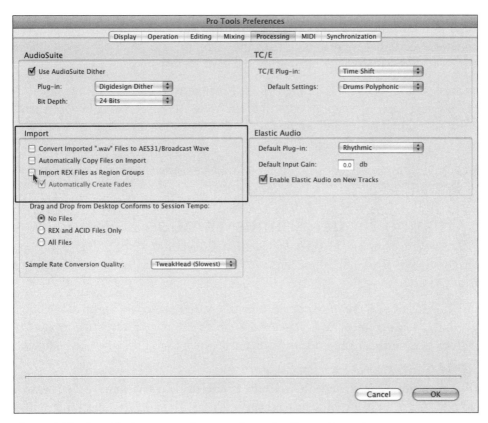

Figure 2.29 REX file import preferences from the Processing tab.

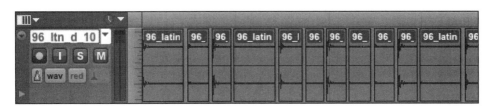

Figure 2.30 Slowing down a REX file imported as a region group will create gaps (for illustration purposes, the REX file was ungrouped).

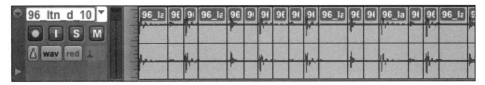

Figure 2.31 Speeding up a REX file imported as a region group will create overlaps (for illustration purposes, the REX file was ungrouped).

In many cases, these gaps and overlaps don't cause significant problems, and some people even prefer the "strobe-light effect" that is created by the gaps. Also, there is no direct processing of the audio. All of the time adjustments are created by the gaps and overlaps.

With that, this tutorial comes to a close, although you are just getting started with understanding tempo. When you next look at tempo, you will learn about the differences between tick-based and sample-based tracks, how to add tempo ramps to your session, and scaling the session tempo to enforce a program-length restriction.

For now, however, you'll turn your sights on creating custom sounds using the library of instruments that comes with Pro Tools 8.

Tutorial 7: Creating Bigger Sounds Through Layering

This tutorial takes advantage of the Pro Tools Creative Collection of virtual instruments, which are included with Pro Tools 8. These include Boom, DB-33, Mini Grand, Structure Free, Vacuum, and Xpand!2.

Although the standard patches of these instruments are well crafted and cover many of the common uses, you may find that the sounds are a bit generic. In this section, you learn how to quickly layer the patches from these instruments to give your music your own unique sound—quickly and painlessly.

There are a few ways to layer MIDI data in order to create thick, rich sounds. One way is to assign multiple parts of a multi-timbral instrument (such as Xpand!2) to the same MIDI channel—allowing these parts to respond to the same MIDI data, thus creating a layer.

The other way is to send the same MIDI data to multiple virtual instruments. This can create rich sounds while taking advantage of an instrument's specialty (using the Mini Grand as the piano, while layering in strings from Xpand!, for instance).

In addition to showing you how to create super layered patches, this tutorial also shows how you can archive some of your trademark sounds and import them into any session.

Layering Sounds with a Multi-Timbral Instrument

The easiest way to create a layered sound is to use a multi-timbral instrument and assign the multiple "parts" of the instrument to the same MIDI channel.

For the purposes of this tutorial, you will create a synth pad layered patch with Xpand!2.

Creating a layered sound within a multi-timbral instrument:

1. Create an instrument track and place Xpand!2 on Insert A.

2. Choose Library > 002 Action Pads > Evolution+ for part A (see Figure 2.32).

3. Choose Library > 005 Polysynths > Fear of Changing Lanes+ for part B.

Figure 2.32   Choosing a patch for part A of Xpand!2

4.   Choose Library > 005 Polysynths > D Something2 for part C.

5.   Choose Library > 003 Pad Layers > Bellisimo for part D.

6.   Assign the MIDI channel for all parts 1 (see Figure 2.33).

With the instrument tracks in Notes view, you should be able to click on the notes on the vertical keyboard and hear both patches play back (see Figure 2.34).

Storing Patches for a Multi-Timbral Instrument

Storing the layered patches created with a multi-timbral instrument is very easy to do. The process is identical to storing any type of plug-in preset. One thing worth mentioning, though, is the difference between storing the preset in the root settings folder versus the session folder. How you plan on using this preset might help you decide which folder is the best option.

In general, if you want to access your layered instrument preset from any session on your computer, you should probably store it in the root settings folder. If you move the session to a different computer, though, you may lose access to the settings.

The other option is to store the preset with the session. This will ensure that your presets will move with the session. After storing the settings to the session folder, you will notice that Pro

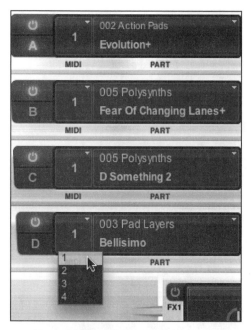

Figure 2.33 Assigning the MIDI channel.

Figure 2.34 Placing a track in Notes view will allow you to play the vertical keyboard and hear Xpand!.

Tools creates a Plug-In Settings folder, which will contain a folder for each specific plug-in that has settings saved.

Setting plug-ins to be saved in a session folder:

1. Click on the Plug-in Settings menu in the plug-in window.

2. Choose Save Plug-in Settings to > Session Folder (see Figure 2.35).

Figure 2.35   Setting plug-ins to be saved to the session folder.

Saving the Plug-in preset:

1.   Click on the Plug-in Settings menu in the plug-in window.

2.   Choose Save Preset As.

3.   Enter Music Production Pad in the Save dialog box (see Figure 2.36).

4.   Click OK.

Figure 2.36   This Save dialog box allows you to save the plug-in.

If you've done this correctly, you should see your new preset available in the Librarian menu in a submenu called Session's Settings Folder (see Figure 2.37).

Figure 2.37 Presets stored in the session folder are found in the Session's Settings Folder submenu of the Librarian menu.

Layering Sounds Using Multiple MIDI Outputs

Although the previous section showed you a quick way to create a layered sound by merely assigning multiple parts to the same MIDI channel, the main limitation is that both layers are required to be parts in the same instrument. What if you wanted to use multiple instruments to create the layers in your sounds? Well, fortunately, Pro Tools has a nifty way to accomplish that without much additional effort.

For this tutorial, you create a "piano and strings" patch that takes advantage of Mini Grand and Xpand!2 plug-ins. Because this layer is comprised of two virtual instruments, it can be confusing to use instrument tracks (although it is possible). To keep the routing clean and easy to follow, you will use Aux and MIDI tracks.

Creating a layered sound with multiple virtual instruments:

1.   With the Mix window showing, create one MIDI track and two stereo Aux tracks.

Figure 2.38 The piano and strings MIDI track with associated Aux tracks. (Note that Pro Tools automatically removes vowels from your track name if space becomes an issue.)

2.   Name the tracks the following (also shown in Figure 2.38):

  MIDI Track: Piano & String MIDI

  Aux 1: Piano

  Aux 2: Strings

3.   On the Insert A of the Piano Aux track, choose RTAS > Instruments > Mini Grand.

4.   On Insert A of the Strings Aux track, choose RTAS > Instruments > Xpand!2. Because there is the second Xpand!2 you are using in this session, take note of its MIDI node (shown in Figure 2.39).

5.   Choose 014 Strings > Big Legato Strings from the Xpand!2 Librarian menu.

6.   From the Output Selector of the MIDI track, choose the Mini Grand node.

Figure 2.39 Knowing the MIDI node will aid in routing MIDI within a session where a virtual instrument is used multiple times.

7.   Press and hold the Control key. Then, choose Xpand!2 from the Output Selector of the MIDI. Be sure to choose the Xpand!2 node that you noted earlier; otherwise this MIDI data might be routed to the Xpand! pad.

You should notice a + sign displayed in the Output Selector (shown in Figure 2.40).

This indicates that the MIDI data is being output to multiple destinations. With the MIDI track in Notes view, you should be able to click on the notes on the vertical keyboard and hear both instruments play back.

Storing Layered "Patches" for Future Use

Although Pro Tools has an effective routing system that allows you to layer sounds with near infinite possibilities, it can be quite a challenge to archive all of this work to be used in future projects. Even though it turns out that there is no dedicated Pro Tools function that will help you

Figure 2.40 The plus sign indicates that this track output is routed to multiple places.

solve this dilemma, there are features that are open ended enough to fit the bill quite well. In a way, this is more of a "store/recall" strategy than taking advantage of a specific feature, as such.

First, you need to save your existing session and create a new library session.

Saving your project session and creating the library session:

1.   Save your current session.

2.   Choose File > Close Session to close the session.

3.   Create a new session (48 kHz sample rate and 24-bit) and name it "Patch Library 1."

Next, you are going to import the layered, virtual instrument tracks from your project session into your library session.

Importing virtual instrument tracks into the library session:

1. With the Patch Library 1 session open, choose File > Import > Session Data.

2. In the Import Session Data dialog box, under Source, select the following tracks:

    Piano & Strings MIDI track

    Piano Aux track

    Strings Aux track

3. The destination will change from None to New Track, as shown in Figure 2.41. Click OK.

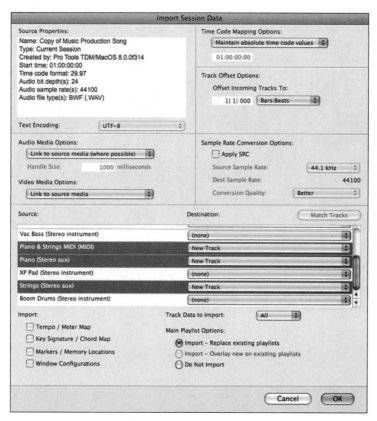

Figure 2.41   Importing tracks from the music production session into the library session.

At this point, you should see the tracks from your project session. By deactivating the tracks, you have effectively told Pro Tools not to factor them in to the session's track limits. This means that you can continue to add tracks to the library session until you feel that it is becoming too unwieldy (in which case, you can just create more sessions to organize all of your sounds). Until then, however, you will certainly appreciate having all of your trademark sounds in a single session (nothing kills the creative vibe like opening session after session with the hope of finding that perfect sound you created that one day when you were just goofing around).

Now that you have a system in place to store all of your layered sounds, finding the perfect custom sound in the future is only a matter of importing the relevant tracks from the archive session. Fortunately, the process of bringing these sounds into your project is really no different from the process you used to store the sound in the first place.

Importing a layered sound from your library session:

1. With your music production session open, choose File > Import > Session Data.

2. In the Import Session Data dialog box, under Source, select the tracks that you want to store. When selected, the destination will change from None to New Track.

3. Click OK.

Of course, because you already have these tracks in your session, you really didn't need to import them again, but now you know how to import these tracks into your next project. You may want to delete the duplicate tracks before continuing.

As a side note, Pro Tools HD users have even more powerful features in the Import Session dialog box. For instance, you can import only select track data, such as plug-in settings or routing. Furthermore, you can import and apply session data to tracks that exist in your current session.

Tutorial 8: Creating and Arranging MIDI-Based Loops

At this point, you have created the song structure, set the initial tempo, conformed audio to match tempo, and created some really interesting patches. Here, you use the Event list, along with the MIDI Editor window, to quickly create some MIDI loops.

After creating some MIDI loops, you will see some ways to quickly lay out and arrange the loops to form a basic arrangement of your song.

Creating Loops with the Event List

The Event list can be an intimidating window to come across (see Figure 2.42). There is nothing like a long list of numbers to really kill the creative moment. As such, it is usually relegated to the "do not use" list for all of eternity. Well, maybe that is an exaggeration, but the MIDI Event list is considerably underused. With that said, this isn't going to be a comprehensive look at how the MIDI Event list will change the way you compose with MIDI, but it can come in handy for quickly and precisely entering notes.

There are many virtual instruments (mostly percussion) that will play a loop as long as a note is held down—Boom is one of them. Although you can simply draw in the note where you want it to be played, you might find it easier to enter the note start and duration into the Event list and be done with it.

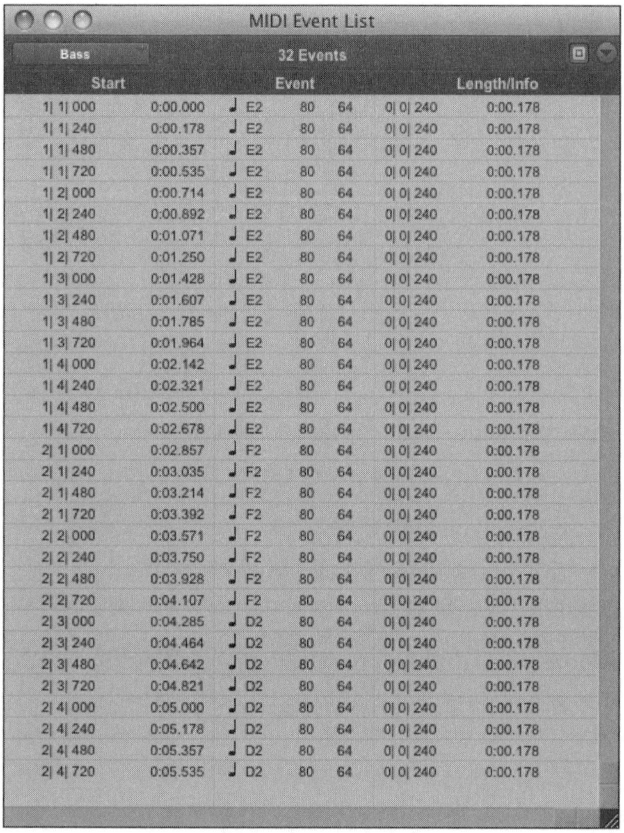

Start		Event			Length/Info	
1| 1| 000	0:00.000	♩ E2	80	64	0| 0| 240	0:00.178
1| 1| 240	0:00.178	♩ E2	80	64	0| 0| 240	0:00.178
1| 1| 480	0:00.357	♩ E2	80	64	0| 0| 240	0:00.178
1| 1| 720	0:00.535	♩ E2	80	64	0| 0| 240	0:00.178
1| 2| 000	0:00.714	♩ E2	80	64	0| 0| 240	0:00.178
1| 2| 240	0:00.892	♩ E2	80	64	0| 0| 240	0:00.178
1| 2| 480	0:01.071	♩ E2	80	64	0| 0| 240	0:00.178
1| 2| 720	0:01.250	♩ E2	80	64	0| 0| 240	0:00.178
1| 3| 000	0:01.428	♩ E2	80	64	0| 0| 240	0:00.178
1| 3| 240	0:01.607	♩ E2	80	64	0| 0| 240	0:00.178
1| 3| 480	0:01.785	♩ E2	80	64	0| 0| 240	0:00.178
1| 3| 720	0:01.964	♩ E2	80	64	0| 0| 240	0:00.178
1| 4| 000	0:02.142	♩ E2	80	64	0| 0| 240	0:00.178
1| 4| 240	0:02.321	♩ E2	80	64	0| 0| 240	0:00.178
1| 4| 480	0:02.500	♩ E2	80	64	0| 0| 240	0:00.178
1| 4| 720	0:02.678	♩ E2	80	64	0| 0| 240	0:00.178
2| 1| 000	0:02.857	♩ F2	80	64	0| 0| 240	0:00.178
2| 1| 240	0:03.035	♩ F2	80	64	0| 0| 240	0:00.178
2| 1| 480	0:03.214	♩ F2	80	64	0| 0| 240	0:00.178
2| 1| 720	0:03.392	♩ F2	80	64	0| 0| 240	0:00.178
2| 2| 000	0:03.571	♩ F2	80	64	0| 0| 240	0:00.178
2| 2| 240	0:03.750	♩ F2	80	64	0| 0| 240	0:00.178
2| 2| 480	0:03.928	♩ F2	80	64	0| 0| 240	0:00.178
2| 2| 720	0:04.107	♩ F2	80	64	0| 0| 240	0:00.178
2| 3| 000	0:04.285	♩ D2	80	64	0| 0| 240	0:00.178
2| 3| 240	0:04.464	♩ D2	80	64	0| 0| 240	0:00.178
2| 3| 480	0:04.642	♩ D2	80	64	0| 0| 240	0:00.178
2| 3| 720	0:04.821	♩ D2	80	64	0| 0| 240	0:00.178
2| 4| 000	0:05.000	♩ D2	80	64	0| 0| 240	0:00.178
2| 4| 240	0:05.178	♩ D2	80	64	0| 0| 240	0:00.178
2| 4| 480	0:05.357	♩ D2	80	64	0| 0| 240	0:00.178
2| 4| 720	0:05.535	♩ D2	80	64	0| 0| 240	0:00.178

Figure 2.42 A busy MIDI Event list.

In order to take advantage of this feature, you need an instrument track with Boom or any other instrument that plays a loop when one note is pressed. If you created a template in the previous chapter, you should already have a Boom track created. If not, create an instrument track and place Boom on it before continuing.

With the Boom track created, let's show the MIDI Event list. Additionally, let's get rid of the Sub Counter in order to make it easier to read.

Showing the MIDI Event list for the Boom instrument track:

1. Select the Boom instrument track.
2. Press Option+= (equals) to open the MIDI Event list.
3. From the MIDI Event List menu, uncheck Show Sub Counter (see Figure 2.43). This will remove it from the window.

Figure 2.43   Removing the Sub Counter will limit the numbers displayed in the MIDI Event list.

Now you can insert a note directly into the MIDI Event list.

Inserting a note on the Boom instrument track through the Event list:

1.   Press Command+N to insert a note into the Event list.

2.   Use the arrow keys to move between fields and enter the following information (see Figure 2.44):

Figure 2.44   A 4-bar note takes up considerably less space in the MIDI Event list than in a graphic editor.

Start: 1 | 1 | 000

Event: C3 120 64 (Note, Attack Velocity, and Release Velocity)

Length/Info: 4 | 1 | 000

3.   Press Enter to lock in the note.

There you have it! You just created a 4-bar loop in your session as easy as that. Since Boom assigns a different pattern to your MIDI note, you can create some variety by just changing the note value from C3 to D3 or E♭3. In fact, you can make one note three bars long and then have a different note for the fourth bar (see Figure 2.45).

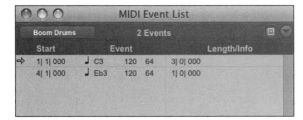

Figure 2.45   Here is a 4-bar loop with a different pattern triggered on the fourth bar.

Creating MIDI Loops in the MIDI Editor Window

Although there are easier ways to get music phrases onto a MIDI track within Pro Tools, they most often require the use of a MIDI controller (many of these ways, such as step recording, recording with Input Quantize, and recording with Loop Playback and MIDI Merge, are covered in the next chapter). With that said, there may be a time when you find yourself away from your studio, and the need arises to enter MIDI data. Fortunately, you can quickly draw and edit notes within the MIDI editor.

To open the MIDI Editor window, you can do either of these:

- Choose Window > MIDI Editor

- Double-click on a MIDI region with the Grabber tool in the Edit window

---

TIP: By default, Pro Tools will open the MIDI Editor window when you double-click on a MIDI region with the Grabber tool. You can change this to have Pro Tools open the Score Editor, MIDI Event list, or even the Region Rename dialog box by clicking on the MIDI tab of the Preferences dialog box and selecting the appropriate action for the Double-Click a MIDI Region Opens preference.

The MIDI Editor window (shown in Figure 2.46) is very similar to the Edit window in that it has Tools and Modes at the top and the Tracks list on the left. One difference is that the Tracks list has an extra column on the right that contains a Pencil icon (shown in Figure 2.47).

This is important to make note of, as Pro Tools allows you to superimpose all of the session MIDI data in the same editor, and the Pencil indicator in the Tracks list lets you know which track you are editing. Also, just like the Edit window, the dot to the left of the track name controls which track's data is actually being shown in the editor.

With the editor open, you can now use the Pencil tool to create a bassline. The Pencil is an intelligent tool. With use of modifier keys and hovering over different parts of a MIDI event, you can do many of the most common editing functions without having to constantly switch between multiple tools. For now, however, you will just be using it to enter notes; Chapter 4 will get more into using the editing aspects of the Pencil tool.

First, let's use the Line Pencil tool to create a note-repeating bassline.

Creating a bassline:

1. In the MIDI Editor, click on the Edit column of the Bass track in the Tracks list.

2. Click and hold on the Pencil tool and choose the Line Pencil (shown in Figure 2.48).

3. Set the Grid value to 1/16 note (shown in Figure 2.49). The grid value tells Pro Tools how often to repeat the note when using the Line Pencil.

Figure 2.46   The MIDI Editor window.

Figure 2.47   The Pencil icon to the right of the track name indicates which MIDI track's data you are editing, whereas the dot to the left indicates which MIDI track's data is showing.

4.   Find E2 and drag a line of notes that spans bar 1 (shown in Figure 2.50).

5.   Find F2 and drag a line of notes that spans the first two beats of bar 2.

6.   Find D2 and drag a line of notes that spans the last two beats of bar 2.

Your bassline should look like Figure 2.51. Next, add the snare roll to the Boom tracks using the same method.

Figure 2.48   Click and hold the Pencil tool to see all its options.

Creating a snare roll from bars 9 through 12 on the Boom track:

1.   In the MIDI Editor, click on the Edit column of the Boom track in the Tracks list.

2.   Scroll until you see bars 9–13 in the MIDI editor. Adjust your zoom level if necessary.

3.   Find E1 and drag a line of notes that spans from 9|1|000 to 13|1|000 (shown in Figure 2.52).

Now, let's quickly add some notes on the piano and strings track. This time, you don't want the notes to repeat, so you need to switch to the Standard Pencil, which allows you to create notes of any length.

Adding the piano and strings accompaniment:

1.   Click on the Edit column of the piano and strings track in the Tracks list (shown in Figure 2.53).

2.   Click and hold the Pencil tool and choose the Standard Pencil.

3.   Find B2 and drag a note that spans bar 1.

Figure 2.49   Click and hold the grid display to choose the grid value.

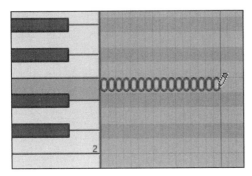

Figure 2.50   The Line Pencil creates a series of notes spaced at the grid value.

4. Find E3 and drag a note that spans bar 1.

5. Find notes C3 and F3 and drag notes that span the first two beats of bar 2.

6. Find notes A2 and D3 and drag notes that span the last two beats of bar 2.

Your Piano and Strings loop should look like Figure 2.54. Finally, you can add some notes for the Pad.

Figure 2.51   The final bassline loop.

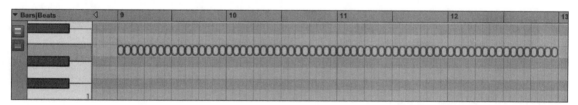

Figure 2.52   A snare roll from bar 9 to bar 13.

Adding notes to trigger the XP Pad track:

1.   Click on the edit column of the Pad track in the Tracks list.

2.   Find E3 and E4 and drag a note that spans bar 1.

3.   Find C4 and drag a note that spans bar 2.

The final XP Pad MIDI data is shown in Figure 2.55.

That's it! You now have four MIDI tracks that all work together. Of course, they are only playing between bars 1 and 2 (except for the snare roll), but you will address that next.

Figure 2.53 Choose the Standard Pencil to create single long notes rather than a series of short ones.

By the way, if you created the template in Chapter 1, you can use the MIDI Editor pane in the Edit window to create the identical types of note input. Although it is convenient to not have to deal with multiple windows, there is something to be said for the larger MIDI editing area in the MIDI Editor window when working with multiple MIDI tracks. In the end, it all comes down to preference.

Quickly Arranging MIDI Regions in the Edit Window

With all of the MIDI data entered, you can close the MIDI Editor window and switch to the Edit window. Notice that the MIDI data is no longer superimposed, and each MIDI track has its own data (see Figure 2.56).

This is going to make it really easy to arrange.

Selecting the Loop Trim tool, and then enabling the Smart tool:

1. Click and hold on the Trim tool, and then choose Loop Trim from the pop-up menu.

2. Click in the space above the Trim, Selector, and Grabber to engage the Smart tool (shown in Figure 2.57).

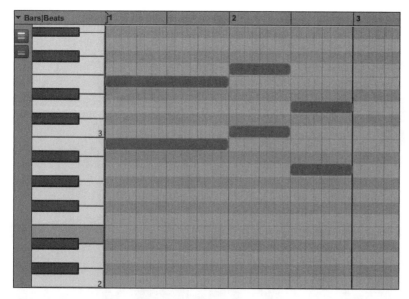

Figure 2.54 The final Piano and Strings loop.

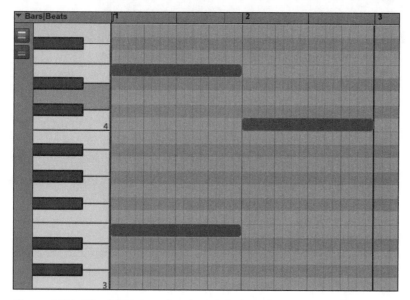

Figure 2.55 The MIDI data for the XP Pad track.

By selecting the Loop Trim tool, you can "paint" out the MIDI region for any duration you need, and with the Smart tool enabled, you can quickly move regions to where you want them to be. This combination of looping and moving allows you to quickly get a rough arrangement your song.

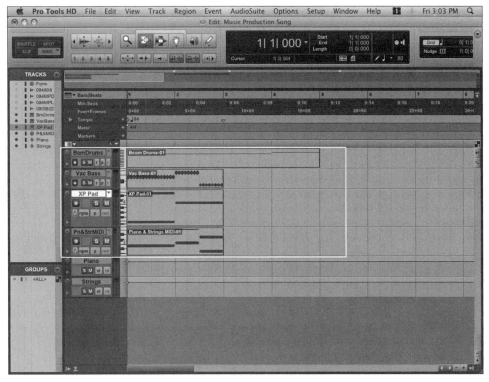

Figure 2.56 The MIDI data is not superimposed in the Edit window.

Putting together a rough arrangement of the MIDI regions for the intro and Section A:

1. Enable Grid mode and assign the Grid to 1 bar.

2. Place the Smart tool at the end of the Boom MIDI region so the Loop Trim tool is visible.

3. Drag the end of the Boom region until it ends at 9 | 1 | 000.

4. Repeat for the Bass track.

5. Place the Smart tool in the middle-upper half of the Piano and Strings region, and drag it so it starts at bar 3 | 1 | 000. Then use the loop trim to extend the region until bar 9 | 1 | 000.

For the outro, you will use many of the same elements used in Section A. Since you are already set up for arranging, why not lay out the outro now?

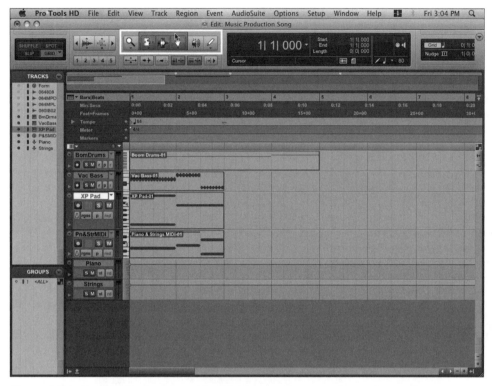

Figure 2.57   Enable the Smart tool by clicking on the area above the toolbar.

Arrange the outro with elements from Section A, as follows:

Region	Start	End
Piano and Strings	22|1|000	31|1|000
XP Pad	22|1|000	30|1|000
Bass	22|1|000	26|1|000

Option+drag the region to create a copy at the start time, and then use Loop Trim to extend them to their relative end times.

Arranging the Audio Files for Intro, Section A, and Outro

Let's finish this tutorial by arranging the drum loops that you imported earlier. Feel free to arrange them how you like. The following table shows how they are arranged in Figure 2.58:

Regions (Intro and Section A)	Start	End
084 Hip Hop Kick (Intro and Section A)	1|1|000	9|1|000
084 MP Distorted Drums (Intro and Section A)	1|1|000	9|1|000
084 MP Latin Jazz Drums (Intro and Section A)	3|1|000	9|1|000
080 Indian Basstabla 02	5|1|000	13|1|000

Regions (Outro)	Start	End
084 Hip Hop Kick	22|1|000	26|1|000
084 MP Distorted Drums	21|1|000	28|1|000
084 MP Latin Jazz Drums	21|1|000	28|1|000
080 Indian Basstabla 02	21|1|000	26|1|000

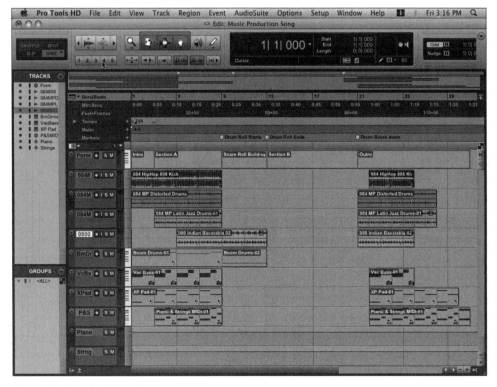

Figure 2.58 The final MIDI and audio arrangement.

Tutorial 9: Adding Dynamic Tempo Changes to Your Session

One of the great design philosophies built into Pro Tools has been to provide the users with as many editing capabilities in as few windows as possible. For a long time, users didn't (and for the most parts, still don't) have to look farther than the Edit or Mix window to accomplish a given task.

This single window philosophy has proven to be a duel-edged sword, of sorts. Although it provides a convenient user interface, it can also create some challenges when you're adjusting the session tempo while working with standard audio (which is based in sample time, aka *absolute time*) and standard MIDI (which is based in ticks, aka *relative time*).

The crux of the problem is caused by how these two timebases fundamentally interact with each other. Understanding this, the program's developer created a simple but elegant solution—allow the users to choose which timebase a track should pay attention to. Although you may be scratching your head, don't worry, it will all start to make sense in the next section. For now, just know that Pro Tools will allow you to select a ticks timebase for audio tracks and, if you desire, choose samples for MIDI tracks. Why you want to do this is the subject of the next section.

Differences Between Tick and Sample Timebases

Although the focus of this tutorial is on working with tempo, it is important to understand the main difference between tick and sample timebases, as your tracks can respond in radically different ways, depending on which timebase it is looking at.

Pro Tools is always keeping track of two different types of time in your session—absolute and relative. The magic link between these two timebases is tempo. In cases where Pro Tools is only used in conjunction with absolute time (sound for film, for instance), the tempo and bars | beats | ticks counters are irrelevant. As such, all of the tracks in a "sound for film" session can be set to samples, and any tempo changes in the session have no effect on the audio in the tracks.

Music, on the other hand, is divided into beats at the rate of the tempo. Although the tempo may change over the duration of the session, absolute time, like minutes and seconds, cannot (think about how hard it would be to keep your appointments if minutes and seconds sped up or slowed down). As such, the relationship between the beats | ticks ruler and any of the absolute rulers needs to be recalculated every time the tempo changes.

For instance, if the tempo is 60 beats per minute, a beat will occur every second (60 beats per minute divided by 60 seconds per minute equals one beat per second). If the tempo is 120 beats per minute, however, the relationship between the ticks and samples needs to be recalculated in order to find that now two beats happen every second (120 beats per minute divided by 60 seconds in a minute equals two beats per second).

Fortunately, Pro Tools will automatically perform these recalculations behind the scenes. The only aspect you have to decide, however, is whether you want samples or ticks to be considered as the "main" timebase when the recalculation is made. Once decided, the track will keep the events (meaning region, automation breakpoint, warp marker, or any other track-based entity) on the track locked to a bar|beat|tick (if the track's timebase is set to Ticks) or a sample, minute, second, or frame (if the track's timebase is set to samples).

I'll illustrate this idea with a more practical example. Let's say you have a session with a tempo of 60 BPM and a region on a vocal track that starts at 5|1|000 (measure 5). If you show both the Bar|Beat and Min:Sec timelines, you will notice that the region starts at 00:16.000 (16 seconds into the session). As long as the tempo is 60 BPM, the vocals will start at measure 5 *and* second 16 (see Figure 2.59).

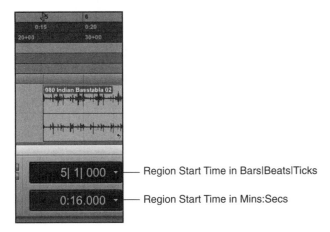

— Region Start Time in Bars|Beats|Ticks
— Region Start Time in Mins:Secs

Figure 2.59   At 60 BPM a region that starts at 5|1|000 also starts at 00:16.000.

Increasing the tempo to 120 BPM will require Pro Tools to recalculate the relationship between the samples and ticks timebases. With the tempo change, each bar's duration will only be two seconds long, instead of four. Thus, as shown in Figure 2.60, measure five is at eight seconds in (instead of 16), and when the session is 16 seconds, it will be at measure 10 (instead of 5).

— Region Start Time in Bars|Beats|Ticks
— Region Start Time in Mins:Secs

Figure 2.60   At 120 BPM, 5|1|000 equals 0:08.000 (instead of 0:16.000).

Let's create an example that shows how tempo changes the events on sample-based and tick-based tracks. To start, create a blank session.

Performing this experiment:

1. Hide all tracks in the session except for the 084 Latin Jazz Drums track and the Piano and Strings track (refer to Figure 2.60).

2. Click on the Conductor Track Enable button in the Transport window (refer back to Figure 2.7).

3. Click in the Tempo field in the Transport window and enter a BPM value of 60.

Notice that before you changed the tempo, the tracks were aligned. With the tempo change, however, they now start at different times. This is because audio tracks lock to samples by default, and MIDI tracks lock to ticks by default.

If you look closely at Figure 2.61, you will notice a symbol directly under the voice selector pop-up (the voice selector pop-up is the button usually populated with the letters "dyn"). This first track will have a blue clock under the voice selector (this tells you that the track's timebase is set to samples). The second track has a green metronome, which tells you that this track's timebase is set to ticks.

Figure 2.61 The blue clock represents the samples timebase, whereas the green metronome signifies the ticks timebase.

As a result, the audio is locked to the Min:Secs ruler, whereas the MIDI is locked to Bars | Beats | Ticks.

Before moving on, you should enable the Conductor Track button in the Transport window.

The session tempo is now set to 84 BPM, and the regions should be aligned again. Let's switch the timebase for the 084 Latin Jazz Drums track to ticks and disable the Conductor again in order to change the tempo back to 60 BPM.

Now, you should notice that the audio and MIDI regions are starting at the same time regardless of tempo. Furthermore, if you have Elastic Audio enabled, the audio regions will automatically time-compress and expand to match the new tempos.

Feel free to manually enter new tempos into the Transport window and note how the different timebases adjust the regions on the tracks. When you are ready to move on, show all tracks and enable the Conductor Track button so the session tempo is back to 84 BPM (see Figure 2.62).

Figure 2.62 The Conductor Track button should be enabled, and your session tempo should be at 84 BPM before moving on.

Preparing Your Session for Dynamic Tempo Changes

In order to complete the next sections in this tutorial, you need to lock all tracks to the ticks timebase. In addition, you need to have Pro Tools recalculate the tempos of any audio files, which means that you also need to enable Elastic Audio on all audio tracks. If you are running a slower computer, you may need also to enable Rendered Processing in order to avoid any errors.

Setting all of the tracks in your session to ticks and enabling Elastic Audio:

1. Option+click on the any track's timebase selection and choose Ticks (shown in Figure 2.63).

2. Option+click on the Elastic Audio Plug-in selector of any track and select Polyphonic.

    Optional: On slower computers, Option+click the Elastic Audio Plug-in selector of any track and select Rendered Processing (shown in Figure 2.64).

Your session is now ready to handle any type of tempo manipulation that you can throw at it!

Adding Tempo Ramps to Your Session

With all of your tracks locked to the ticks timebase and Elastic Audio enabled, your session is prepared to handle even the most demanding tempo shifts, all the while keeping everything locked to its place in the music.

This makes for an ideal time to create a basic tempo map that includes a tempo ramp (and an additional tempo event). Let's start by creating a 4-bar tempo ramp that starts at 84 BPM and speeds up to 168 BPM (doubling the original tempo).

Figure 2.63 Holding down the Option key while making track adjustments will apply the changes to all tracks in the session.

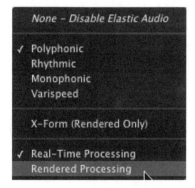

Figure 2.64 Enabling Rendered Processing will help you out if you are working with a slower computer.

Creating a tempo ramp over the Snare Roll Section of the song:

1.   Click on the Snare Roll region in the Form track (see Figure 2.65).

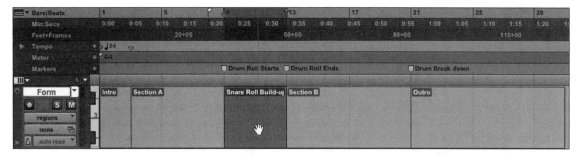

Figure 2.65 Using the Form track is a quick way to make time selections in your session.

2. Choose Event > Tempo Operations > Parabolic.

3. Type "168" in the Tempo End field.

4. Set Curvature to 23.

5. Uncheck the Preserve Tempo after Selection checkbox.

6. If your Tempo Operations window looks like Figure 2.66, click Apply.

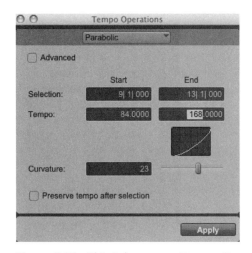

Figure 2.66 This is how your Tempo Operations window should look.

You should see a bunch of tempo events in the Tempo Ruler, as well as a change in the length of regions (shown in Figure 2.67). Now, you should notice that the snare roll (and any regions playing) speeds up as the tempo is increased.

Next, let's bring the tempo back down to 84 at the outro. There are a couple of ways to do this, but the easiest is just to insert a single tempo event at the start of the outro.

Figure 2.67   Tempo events added to the Tempo Ruler.

Setting the tempo of the outro to be 84 BPM:

1.   With the Grabber, click on the Outro region on the Form track.

2.   Click on the + in the Tempo Ruler (shown in Figure 2.68).

Figure 2.68   This plus sign adds a single tempo event.

3.   Type "84" in the BPM field. The location should already be set to 21 | 1 | 000.

4.   If your Tempo Change dialog box looks like Figure 2.69, click OK.

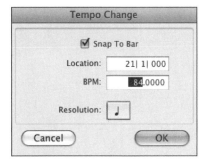

Figure 2.69 This is how your Tempo Change dialog box should look.

That is how you create a quick tempo map that can add a bit of interest to your song.

At this point, why not take some time and build up Section B using the information that was covered up (find, import, create and arrange loops, MIDI data, maybe even add in some more tempo changes)? Feel free to add as many tracks as you need. When you are ready to move on, you will learn about conforming the entire piece of music to fit a specific length.

Using Tempo to Conform a Music Cue to a Specific Duration

There may be times when you will need to fit your music into a specific timeframe. For instance, many production music libraries require music to conform to standard lengths used in advertising (such as 30-, 60-, and 90-second lengths). Odds are that your song isn't going to land squarely on any of these lengths (especially if your song has tempo changes of any kind). With Pro Tools, however, this isn't much of a problem. Pro Tools can scale and calculate any and all tempos in your session to fit a given length.

If you go to the end of the Form track (it should be bar 31|1|00) and check the Mins:Secs sub-time scale in the Transport window (shown in Figure 2.70), you will notice that the session ends around 1:12.218. For the purposes of this example, let's say that you need the session to be 1:15.

Figure 2.70 Currently, your song is at 1:12.218, but that is about to change.

Scaling the tempo of the session to fit the length of 1:15:

1. Make sure that the main timescale is set to Bars | Beats.

2. Triple-click on the Form track with the selector.

3. Choose Event > Tempo Operations > Scale.

4. Click the Advanced checkbox to show the advanced settings.

5. Choose Average Tempo from the Calculate drop-down box and All Tempos from the Scale drop-down box.

6. In the Mins:Secs End field, type "1:15."

7. Uncheck the Preserve Tempo after Selection checkbox.

8. If your Tempo Operations window looks like Figure 2.71, click Apply.

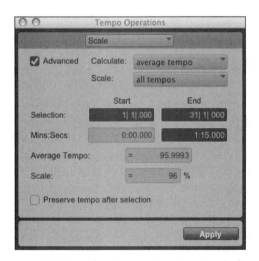

Figure 2.71 The Tempo Operations window should look like this.

You will notice that the tempos have all slowed down a little bit, but your session now ends at exactly 1:15 (shown in Figure 2.72).

Please remember that when dealing with tempo, you should always have Elastic Audio enabled on all audio tracks, and every track in your session should be set to ticks (unless you have specific reasons for them to be in samples). Otherwise, you may find that some tracks will suddenly be out of time with the rest of your session.

Tutorial 10: Maintaining System Performance

If you find yourself using a lot of virtual instruments in your session, you may notice that your session is acting a little sluggish. This is because the host CPU in your computer has to render the

Figure 2.72 Now the session is exactly 1:15.

audio for each virtual instruments in real-time. This happens to take considerably more processing power than simply reading an audio file off of a disk.

As a result, it is a good idea to record the audio from the virtual instruments once you are happy with them. In addition, Pro Tools has a feature that allows you to deactivate tracks so they use zero processing power while still keeping all of the data intact, should you need to get back to it.

Checking System Load

First, it is a good idea to know how to keep an eye on your system's available resources. This is done through the System Usage window (see Figure 2.73). Choose Window > System Usage to view this dialog box.

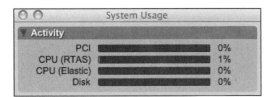

Figure 2.73 The LE System Usage window.

The information contained in the window depends on whether you are using Pro Tools LE or Pro Tools HD (the Pro Tools M-Powered version of this window is identical to LE). If any of these meters start to approach their limits, you will notice a significant performance hit and possibly be presented with an error. So, knowing how much demand you are putting on your system and which components are most impacted allows you to adjust playback settings to get the best performance, while maximizing the use of the processor or processors. Of course, that is only if you understand the meters and know what adjustments to make when activity is too high.

With that said, here are the meters in the System Usage window for Pro Tools LE (shown in Figure 2.73):

- **PCI**—Displays the amount of PCI bus activity.

- **CPU (RTAS)**—Displays the amount of processing activity derived from the RTAS plug-in (both effects and virtual instruments).

- **CPU (Elastic)**—Displays the amount of processing activity derived from the Elastic Audio plug-ins used in your session.

- **Disk**—Displays the current load on your hard disk(s).

In addition to these meters, Pro Tools HD adds the following (shown in Figure 2.74):

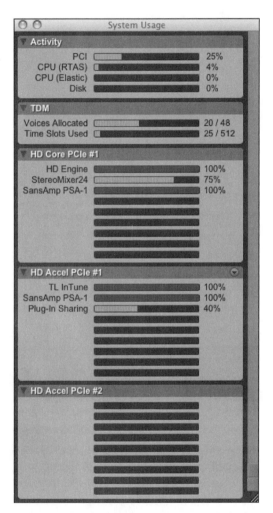

Figure 2.74   The HD System Usage window.

- **TDM Voice Allocation**—Displays the current number out of the total number of disk voices being used.

- **TDM Time Slots**—Displays the current number of TDM time slots used out of the TDM total number of time slots available.

- **DSP Usage**—Displays the amount of activity on each of the available TDM processors. The number of meters depends on the number of cards installed in your system. Each card adds nine additional processors to the HD system.

Optimizing System Load

Now that you can see how your system is performing, you may want to make some adjustments in order to balance the system load. Due to space requirements, only host-based optimizations are covered here.

CPU (RTAS) Meter

If this meter is peaking quite high, or if you are receiving an error like the one shown in Figure 2.75, you might need to make some changes to the playback engine.

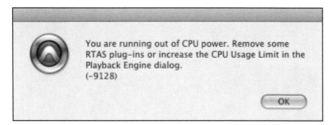

You are running out of CPU power. Remove some RTAS plug-ins or increase the CPU Usage Limit in the Playback Engine dialog.
(-9128)

OK

Figure 2.75 Peaking the CPU may cause an error like this to appear.

Open the Playback Engine dialog box by choosing Setup > Playback Engine.

Within the Playback Engine dialog box there are two main parameters that you should be aware of (shown in Figure 2.76). The first is RTAS Processors, and the second is CPU Usage Limit. These two settings work together to help balance the load of your particular system.

If you have a multi-processor system, you can allocate more processors to be dedicated to RTAS processing. This will allow you to run more plug-ins. A word of caution, though; if you assign all of your available processors to RTAS processing, you may find that other aspects of the software start to get bogged down, such as screen redraws, automation accuracy, and video playback.

CPU Usage Limit determines how much activity can exist on any of the processors. If you find you are getting errors, you can increase the CPU usage limit to take greater advantage of the process-ors. In most cases, it is fine to set it to the maximum if you are not allocating all of your processors to RTAS processing. If you are allocating all of your processors, however, you can use this setting to balance the system performance against RTAS performance. By lowering this limit, you allow other processes (such as screen redraws) to have some room on the processor.

The ideal settings aren't exclusively dependant on your computer, though. There is a lot to be said for the content of the session. For instance, you may have one session with a large number

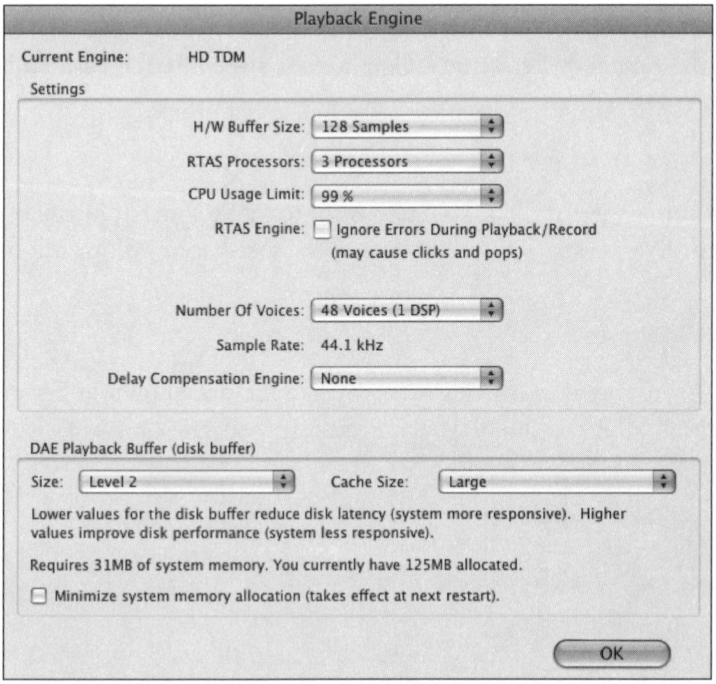

Figure 2.76   The Playback Engine dialog box.

of RTAS plug-ins. To compensate, you may need more dedicated RTAS processors with higher CPU usage limits. Then, you might have another session with a significant amount of automation and HD video. This may require that you reduce both settings—the number of RTAS processors and the CPU usage limit.

CPU (Elastic) Meter

Elastic Audio can really take a toll on slower systems. If you find that this meter is peaking, there are a couple of things you can do.

This first thing you can do is increase the Cache Size of the DAE Buffer (located in the Playback Engine dialog box, shown in Figure 2.77). There isn't a great deal of flexibility here, as you only

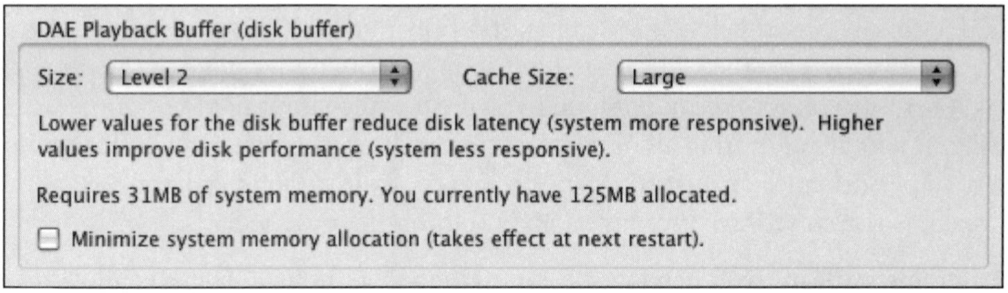

Figure 2.77   DAE Playback Buffer settings in the Playback Engine dialog box.

can choose Minimum, Normal, or Large. With that said, however, it might be enough to keep your session humming along while you finalize your tempo changes.

As discussed in Tutorial 6, the other option is to put some or all of the tracks using Elastic Audio into Rendered Processing mode. In Rendered Processing mode, Pro Tools will take the audio files offline, calculate the tempo changes, and then bring the files back online each time the tempo changes or the TCE trim is used. Although this can definitely break up the flow of things, it is a nice compromise for those who are adjusting tempo and want Pro Tools to do all of the calculations, but don't want to (or can't, due to a slow CPU) allocate real-time DSP to do it.

Disk Meter

When the disk meter peaks, there can be all kinds of trouble that arise—pops and clicks might appear in your audio, or a "Disk Too Slow" error could pop up. Because hard drives store the creative output of the session, it is important that they are as efficient as possible.

Due to their importance, there are a few ways to minimize disk activity. Some of the obvious ones are to buy faster hard drives and keep your disks optimized. Another quick fix is to consolidate all of the edits from your tracks. This is done by selecting all of the regions on a track and choosing Edit > Consolidate Selection (just like you did in the first tutorial of this chapter). Essentially, this rewrites all of the audio data within the selection as a single audio file.

Another way to reduce drive strain is to use multiple hard drives. Although Pro Tools doesn't work well with a RAID disk array, it does have the facilities for recording to and playing back from multiple disks. This is covered in Chapter 3.

Last but not least, you can adjust how much audio the DAE engine buffer is caching. By increasing the buffer, however, you are effectively slowing down the response time of your whole system. This might be a fair trade if none of the other options fits the bill.

Recording Virtual Instrument Output

There are times when your session is so robust that no matter how you optimize, there just isn't enough processing to be found. When this happens, you are left with one option, and that is to record down each of your virtual instrument tracks.

Before getting started, you need to evaluate how many tracks you need to record down. It's really a matter of how much flexibility you want during the mixing process. For instance, if you have a large number of tracks to mix, recording groups of virtual instruments to the same audio track may help make the mix more manageable. The trade-off there is that you won't be able to adjust the blend of those virtual instruments during mixdown. If you find you really need to readjust those tracks, you still have the option of going back to the source tracks later. The inconvenience of going back to mix something again might be worth enough, however, to sacrifice an audio track and just record everything separately.

In addition to determining how flexible you want to be, you also need to have at least one bus (preferably two busses, for stereo) available for each virtual instrument you want to record down. If you are on Pro Tools HD (or LE with Complete Production Toolkit), this shouldn't pose much of a problem, as they each have 128 busses available. Standard Pro Tools LE and M-Powered, however, have 32 busses. This translates to only 16 stereo tracks, assuming that you haven't been using your busses for anything else. If worse comes to worst, you can always do multiple passes to record down all of your instruments.

In the example here, you will record down all of the virtual instruments (Boom, Piano, Strings, and Pad). The Piano and Strings layers will be recorded on two separate tracks, whereas the four layers of the Xpand!2 pad will be mixed and recorded to a single track. Boom, for obvious reasons, will be recorded on it own track. When all is said and done, your session will have only one virtual instrument track remaining—Vac Bass. In Chapter 4, you make some edits to the MIDI data on this track, so it is good that it isn't being recorded down just yet.

Renaming the Busses

To start, you need separate sets of busses for each instrument you are recording down. In this case, you need four stereo pairs of busses (for Piano, Strings, Pad, and Boom). Also, it is important to name your busses to accurately reflect what they are being used for. This will reduce routing errors and ensure a smooth setup.

In addition, a good name will help you recognize busses that are no longer needed because the task they were used for is complete. For instance, once the recording is complete, you probably won't be using these busses for this purpose. By naming them descriptively, you can repurpose them as soon as the need arises.

Renaming the busses to accurately reflect their roles:

1. Choose Setup > I/O Setup.

2. Click on the Bus tab and double-click on Bus 25–26.

3. Type "Piano Rec Bus" to rename the bus.

4. Repeat for Bus 27–28, Bus 29–30, and Bus 31–32.

5. If your window looks like Figure 2.78, click OK.

Creating New Stereo Audio Tracks

Next, you need to create some audio tracks to record the instruments down to.

Creating four new stereo audio tracks, and moving them to the left of each source track in the Mix window:

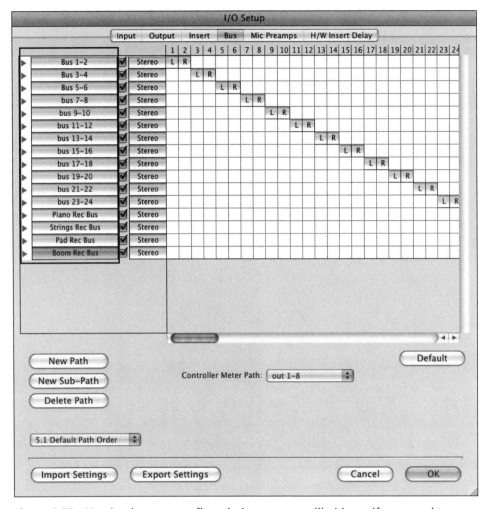

Figure 2.78 Naming busses to reflect their purposes will aid you if you need to repurpose them later.

1. Open the Mix window.

2. Create four new stereo audio tracks. Name them Piano REC, Strings REC, Pad REC, and Boom REC.

3. Select the Piano REC track and move it directly to the right of the Piano Aux track.

4. Move the Strings REC, Pad REC, and Boom REC tracks directly to the right of the Strings Aux and Pad instrument tracks.

If your screen looks like Figure 2.79, you are all set to take care of the routing. Many people prefer to do their routing in the Mix window because it is easier to check for mistakes (all of the

Figure 2.79 At this point, this is how your Mix window should look.

inputs and outputs appear next to each other in a row), although it is possible to do the routing in the I/O view of the Edit window if you prefer.

Routing the Outputs of the VI Tracks

Using the renamed busses to route the outputs of the VI (virtual instrument) tracks to the audio tracks:

1. In the Output Selector of the Piano aux track, choose Bus > Piano Rec.

2. In the Input Selector of the Piano VI audio track, choose Bus > Piano Rec.

3. Repeat the process for the Strings and Pad using the Strings Rec and Pad Rec busses, respectively.

Figure 2.80   This is the Mix window after the routing is complete.

If your Mix window looks like Figure 2.80, you are all set. All you have left to do is make the recording!

Recording the Virtual Instruments

Recording the virtual instruments:

1.   Record-enable the audio tracks.

2.   Press 3 on the numeric keypad to set the transport recording.

There you have it—the output of the virtual instruments is recorded down as audio files (the Edit window is shown in Figure 2.81).

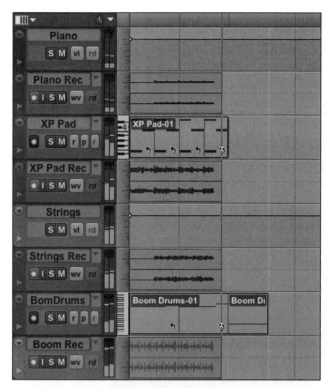

Figure 2.81   Recording down the virtual instruments.

Hiding and Making Tracks Inactive

With the virtual instruments recorded down as audio, the real-time VI tracks are no longer necessary. Although it is possible to just delete them to free up their resources, you might find yourself in a pickle if you later want to modify and re-record them.

A much better way to free up these resources is to make these tracks inactive. By making them inactive, you completely disable them in the session. They will not play back audio, and any plug-ins on inactive tracks will not be actively processed or use session resources of any kind. They are effectively deleted from the session, with one key difference. If you ever need to get back to their data, you can simply make them active again. Presto, your tracks are back to life!

Because MIDI tracks don't take up any significant amount of resources, it isn't possible to make them inactive. It is good practice, however, to hide any MIDI tracks that are associated with virtual instruments that are inactive.

One last note—the following steps illustrate deactivating tracks and hiding tracks as two separate steps. Pro Tools has a Hide and Make Inactive option that effectively combines these two steps into one, but the choice to keep them separate was deliberate, as it allows you to see what inactive tracks look like.

Making the Piano and Stings MIDI, Piano Aux, Strings Aux, XP Pad, and Boom drum instrument tracks inactive and hidden:

1. Select the following tracks in the Mix window:

    Piano and Strings (MIDI track)

    Piano (Aux track)

    Strings (Aux track)

    Pad (Instrument track)

2. While holding Option+Shift, right-click on the Piano Aux track and choose Make Inactive. All of the selected tracks will turn gray (except for the MIDI track), indicating that they are inactive. See Figure 2.82.

3. While holding Option+Shift, right-click on the Piano Aux track and choose Hide Track.

Figure 2.82   Inactive tracks appear gray italics in the Mix and Edit windows.

Now the virtual instrument tracks are no longer using valuable real-time processing. To make an inactive track active again, you simply show the track (by clicking on the track's Show/Hide indicator in the Tracks list), right-click on it, and choose Make Active.

Summary

Phew! This chapter covered a lot of ground. You learned about workflows such as setting up a song structure with skeleton regions to help with editing while freeing up markers for timeline comments and lyrics. You created layers within a single virtual instrument and with multiple virtual instruments, plus created a library session to store your favorite sounds for later use.

Also, you were introduced to some of the static and dynamic tempo features within Pro Tools. Along with that, you saw how to conform the tempo of audio files to the session tempo and had just a taste of what Elastic Audio is about (more to come with Chapter 4).

This led to becoming familiar with the Event list, as well as some of the MIDI editing tools in order to "pencil in" and quickly arrange some MIDI lines even if there was no MIDI controller to be found.

Rounding out the chapter, you learned how to balance the processing power and resources of your machine. After all, with all of the virtual instruments and applications working together, you want to be sure that everything is running at peak efficacy.

Believe it or not, for all that was covered, there is much more to discuss. In short, Pro Tools 8 brings music production to the forefront in a big way. If you are someone who has "made do" with working in multiple applications in the past (using Pro Tools for "engineering" purposes only), now is the time to consider Pro Tools as a single front-end application to get you from scratch tracks to final arrangement.

3 Recording in Pro Tools

Although the physical act of recording can be straightforward, it is common for issues to creep up from time to time. A successful recording session can live or die by the amount of care you take in the setup phase. As such, the large portion of this chapter focuses on setting up for recording. Here you will learn about getting the best hard drive performance, determining whether multiple drives are needed, creating and customizing a click track, setting and adjusting the track input monitor, and reducing latency when recording with Pro Tools LE.

After you have your system set up, you should be able to make standard recordings without much problem. Because the basics in standard linear recording can be found in Chapter 2 (see the section entitled "Recording Virtual Instrument Output"), the focus here will be on a couple of other recording modes: Loop Record and QuickPunch. If you have questions about recording basics, *Pro Tools 101* by Digidesign and Frank D. Cook (ISBN: 1-59863-866-1) is an excellent resource.

Next, this chapter turns your attention to MIDI recording. Chapter 2 showed you how to manually draw in MIDI notes and events, and this chapter focuses on using a MIDI controller as an input. Although using a MIDI controller can certainly speed things up, there is also a certain amount of setup required. You will see how to set the MIDI Thru, enable Input Quantize, take advantage of Step Input, and create complex MIDI sequences with MIDI Merge.

By the end of this chapter, you should feel comfortable diving in and adjusting many of recording-based preferences and options to suit the particular requirements of the recording session.

Tutorial 11: Setting Up to Record Audio

Preparing Pro Tools for a recording session isn't terribly time consuming. With that said, it would be a mistake to not put any thought and planning into it at all. Plus, as recording sessions get larger and more complex, the potential for something to go horribly wrong increases substantially.

In this tutorial, you go "under the hood" of Pro Tools and tweak some preference and options that will ensure that you have a smooth recording session.

Determining Recording Time Based on Disk Space

There can be many comparisons made between digital and analog recorders when thinking about the amount of recording time available. In the case of analog recorders, the amount of recording time is determined by the amount of tape on the reel and the speed at which the recorder is running. So, if the recording is running at 30 inches per second (ips), you have half as much recording time when compared to the same amount of tape running at 15 ips. Of course, the benefit of running at faster tape speeds is that you get a higher quality recording. In either case (running at 15 ips or 30 ips), there is a formula employed that will convert the number of inches of tape to the number of minutes of recording time.

Even though Pro Tools, or any other DAW for that matter, doesn't use tape, they all use some sort of medium. That medium, a hard drive in this case, is still the gating factor that determines maximum record time. Furthermore, there is a formula to convert the total number of megabytes available to the total number of minutes of recording time.

Initially, it can be tricky to determine the amount of recording time available on the drive, due to a number of factors—mainly sample rate and bit depth of the audio being recorded. The general guideline is that it takes 5 MB of disk space to record one minute of mono audio at 44.1 kHz and 16-bit. From there, determining the amount of recording time available for other sample rates and bits is pretty straightforward. If you record at 44.1 kHz and 24-bit, you need to budget an extra 50% disk space (7.5 MB per mono minute), because 24-bit samples are 50% larger than 16-bit samples. If you record at 88.2 and 24-bit, you need to double the budget over the previous example (15 MB per mono minute) because there are twice as many samples in a minute of audio recorded at 88.2 kHz when compared to 44.1 kHz.

These calculations give you a fairly close approximation of the number of recording minutes that are available on your disk. If you don't want to do the math, don't worry! Pro Tools keeps track of the amount of free disk space and even converts it to minutes so you can see how much recording time is available on each drive through the Disk Usage window.

To show the Disk Usage window, choose Window > Disk Space. See Figure 3.1.

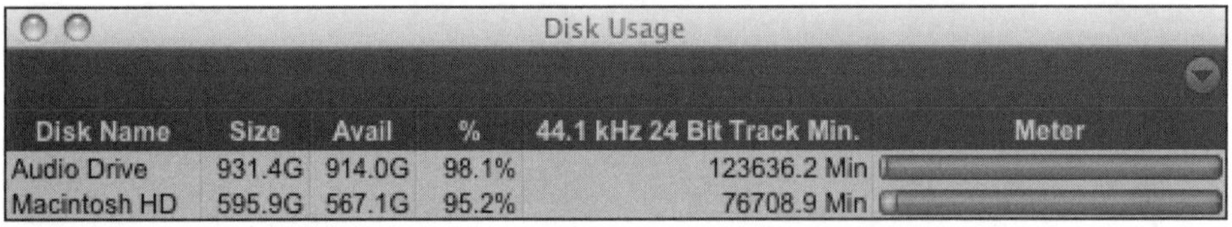

Disk Name	Size	Avail	%	44.1 kHz 24 Bit Track Min.	Meter
Audio Drive	931.4G	914.0G	98.1%	123636.2 Min	
Macintosh HD	595.9G	567.1G	95.2%	76708.9 Min	

Figure 3.1 The Disk Usage window shown with optional meter.

The Disk Usage window (shown in Figure 3.1) shows you statistics based on your current session sample rate and bit depth for each of the drives that are connected to your system. These include:

- Disk name

- Total size

- Available space

- Percentage available

- Total of track minutes (based on your session's sample rate and bit depth)

- A meter showing how much disk space is used (optional)

You may notice that the number of minutes is quite high. It is important to keep in mind that this number reflects the total number of *track* minutes. So if you are recording two mono tracks, you will use two track minutes for each minute of recording. If you are recording 16 mono tracks, you will use 16 track minutes for each minute of recording. If you are recording with stereo tracks, you will need to double the amount of track minutes again (due to stereo tracks being two channels of audio). In that case, 16 stereo tracks will eat up 32 track minutes per minute of recording. As you can see, what seems to be a large number of track minutes can quickly be taken up during a larger recording session.

Limiting Drive Space

By default, Pro Tools is set to open-ended recording. This means that if you start recording a track and never press Stop, Pro Tools will continue to record until all available space is used up. Although this is a safe bet if you are recording a long program, it does come at a cost. With all available drive space allocated, Pro Tools may take a little longer to start recording. Open-ended drive allocation will also cause your drives to work harder. If you are working on a large recording session, with many musicians in the studio and clients over your shoulder, the last thing you want to do is give your drives something to complain about.

You can increase Pro Tools' performance, while simultaneously reducing the load on your hard drives, by limiting the amount of time that Pro Tools can record in one pass.

Limiting the amount of recording time per pass to 60 minutes:

1. Choose Setup > Preferences.

2. Click on the Operation tab.

3. From the Open-Ended Record Allocation section, click the Limit To radio button.

4. Type "60" in the Limit To text field, shown in Figure 3.2, to limit this to 60 minutes.

5. Click OK.

With the drive allocation set to 60 minutes, each track can record up to 60 minutes of audio before Pro Tools stops. This applies to all recording modes, including loop recording (discussed later). So if you are loop recording over a one-minute section, you will have 60 passes, after which Pro Tools will stop and throw the error shown in Figure 3.3. Make sure that the time limit is longer than the expected recording (it would be tragic to have an inspiring recording cut short due to an incorrectly set artificial limit). The idea is to tell Pro Tools there is a limit, but have the limit far out enough that there isn't a chance of ever really reaching it. Also, it is

Pro Tools Preferences

Display | Operation | Editing | Mixing | Processing | MIDI | Synchronization

Transport

☐ Timeline Insertion/Play Start Marker Follows Playback
☐ Edit Insertion Follows Scrub/Shuttle
☐ Audio During Fast Forward/Rewind
☐ Latch Forward/Rewind
☑ Play Start Marker Follows Timeline Selection
☐ Reserve Voices For Preview In Context

Custom Shuttle Lock Speed: 800 %
Back/Forward Amount:
    2I 0I 000 | Bars|Beats ⬍

Numeric Keypad:
    ○ Classic
    ⦿ Transport   ☐ Use Separate Play and Stop Keys
    ○ Shuttle

Auto Backup

☑ Enable Session File Auto Backup
            Keep: 10   most recent backups
        Backup every: 5   minutes

Video

QuickTime Playback Priority: Medium ⬍
☐ High Quality QuickTime Image

Record

☑ Latch Record Enable Buttons
☑ Link Record and Play Faders
☑ Audio Track RecordLock
☐ Transport RecordLock
☑ Disable "Input" when Disarming Track (In "Stop")
☐ Mute Record-Armed Tracks while Stopped
☐ PEC/Direct Style Input Monitoring
☐ Automatically Create New Playlists When Loop Recording

Online Options:
    ⦿ Record Online at Time Code (or ADAT) Lock
    ○ Record Online at Insertion/Selection

Open-Ended Record Allocation:
    ○ Use All Available Space
    ⦿ Limit to: 60   minutes

DestructivePunch File Length: 25   minutes

Misc

☑ Show Quick Start dialog when Pro Tools starts
Auto Region Fade In/Out Length: 0   msec
Calibration Reference Level: -   18   dB

[Cancel]   [OK]

Figure 3.2 The Open-Ended Record Allocation preference section of the Operation tab.

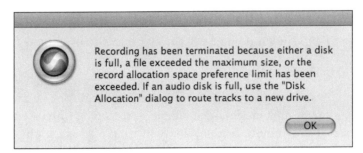

Recording has been terminated because either a disk is full, a file exceeded the maximum size, or the record allocation space preference limit has been exceeded. If an audio disk is full, use the "Disk Allocation" dialog to route tracks to a new drive.

[OK]

Figure 3.3 This error message will appear when your drive is full or when Pro Tools reaches the recording limit you set.

important to note that this setting doesn't prevent Pro Tools from running out of disk space, so be sure to keep an eye on the Disk Usage window!

Recording to Multiple Hard Drives

Another important factor when setting up for a record session is the number of drives required. If you are recording a sample rate of 48 kHz or less and are recording or playing back fewer than 24 tracks, one drive should be sufficient. It is highly recommended that this drive *not* be the system or boot drive of your computer (see the sidebar entitled "Use a Separate Drive for Your Audio Files" for more information).

If you are recording at a higher sample rate or have an increased track count, you should probably consider adding one or more drives. Having more drives means that you'll have more mechanisms to record, seek, and queue audio data. Table 3.1 shows the number of tracks that can play back from a given number of drives at a given sample rate. Of course, these are just suggestions. The number of edits per second (known as *edit density*) on each track can significantly change the number of drives required to play a session back.

Table 3.1 Number of Tracks per Drive and Sample Rate

Drives	44.1/48 kHz	96 kHz	192 kHz
1	24	12	6
2	48	24	12
3	72	36	18
4	96	48	24
5	120	60	30
6	128	72	36
8	192	96	36

Use a Separate Drive for Your Audio Files Operating systems prefer to have a lot of free drive space for optimum performance. If the system drive fills up during a recording session, a tug-of-war of sorts is created between the operating system and Pro Tools, where both are fighting for the same disk space to accomplish the same goal—to record your audio. In the end, if the space gets all used up, no one wins. Pro Tools will throw a "disk full" error (refer to Figure 3.3) a second before the OS crashes.

In the best case, you may have plenty of disk space, and there is no threat of running out during the session. You may not have a problem recording (although Avid doesn't support this configuration), and all will be fine in a pinch. The problem, however, involves maintenance and organization. Plus, your session could be in jeopardy if your computer gets a virus or you need to reformat and re-install your operating system.

By keeping your audio on a separate drive, you're not only getting the best performance out of your system, but also keeping a degree of separation between the computer and your creative content.

If your session is using multiple drives, you can choose to assign each track to a specific drive. This is done from the Disk Allocation dialog box.

Showing the Disk Allocation dialog box:

1. Open a template or create and name the desired number of tracks that you will be recording.

2. Choose Setup > Disk Allocation. The Disk Allocation dialog box, shown in Figure 3.4, lists all of the session's audio tracks.

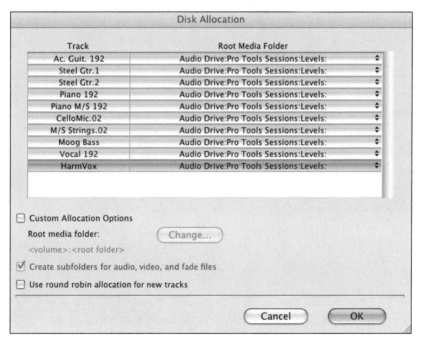

Figure 3.4 The Disk Allocation dialog box.

Directly to the right of the track name, the path where the audio will be recorded (known as the Root Media folder) is identified. Below it, you will see a few options such as customizing the default root media folder or enabling round robin for all newly created tracks.

3.   Click on the track's path in the Root Media Folder column, shown in Figure 3.5, to change the disk allocation for that track.

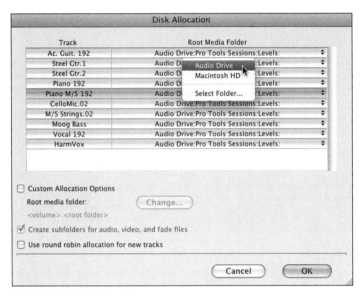

Figure 3.5   Click in the Root Media Folder column for each track to change the record drive.

In Figure 3.5, you can see that first couple of menu choices are drives that are available for recording. By choosing a drive, you are *not* telling Pro Tools to record to the root level of the hard disk, but rather identifying the drive where Pro Tools will create a session folder (with the same name as the current session) and an audio files folder where the audio files will reside. You can override this by choosing the Select Folder menu option.

There are a couple of conditions for a drive to show up in the list. First, it needs to have available space for recording. Second, it needs to be designated as an audio drive. Later in the chapter, you will learn to designate a drive as a Record, Playback, or Transfer volume. For now, it should suffice to say you won't see any drive that isn't a record-designated volume. That means you won't see any CD or Flash drives in the list (these are automatically designated as Transfer volumes).

If you want Pro Tools to automatically assign a different drive to each new audio track that is created in your session you can enable the round robin setting. To enable round robin recording for newly created tracks, you click the checkbox in the bottom of the Disk Allocation dialog box (see Figure 3.6).

The round robin option allows all new tracks to be democratically divided among all available audio drives by assigning each track to a separate drive until all drives are assigned. Then, it repeats the process indefinitely until all tracks are assigned. For instance, if you have four drives and 16 audio tracks, each drive will be responsible for four tracks. The first drive will have tracks 1, 5, 9, and 13. The second drive will have tracks 2, 6, 10, and 14. The third drive

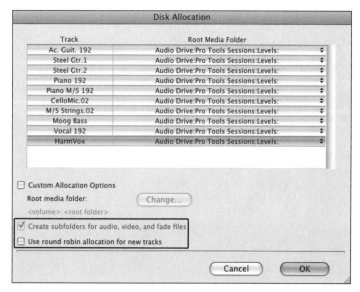

Figure 3.6 The Use Round Robin checkbox.

will start will with track 3 and have every fourth track, and the fourth drive will start with track 4. This allows all four drives to evenly bear the burden of the session.

Changing Drive Designation

A volume can have one of three designations: Record, Playback, or Transfer. As a Record drive, Pro Tools will use the drive to record, play back, and transfer audio files. If it is designated as a Playback drive, Pro Tools will not use it to record, but it will still use it for playing back audio and transferring data. Although a session opened on a Playback drive will play fine, any newly recorded audio files will be recorded on a record-designated volume.

By changing the designation of a Record drive to Playback or Transfer, you prevent it from showing up in the Disk Allocation dialog box, thereby preventing Pro Tools from being able to record to it.

Designating your system drive as Playback only:

1. Choose Window > Workspace (or press Option-;) to open the Workspace browser.

2. Choose Playback from the pop-up menu in the A of the system drive (see Figure 3.7).

3. If you open a session from a drive designated as Transfer Only (such as read-only media like a DVD, or from a network storage drive), you will get the message shown in Figure 3.8. By clicking OK in this dialog box, you will be directed to the Save Copy In dialog box, where you can choose to save your session and its related data on an appropriate drive.

Every drive volume that is mounted when Pro Tools is running has one of these designations. The default designations assigned by Pro Tools are usually adequate for standard applications.

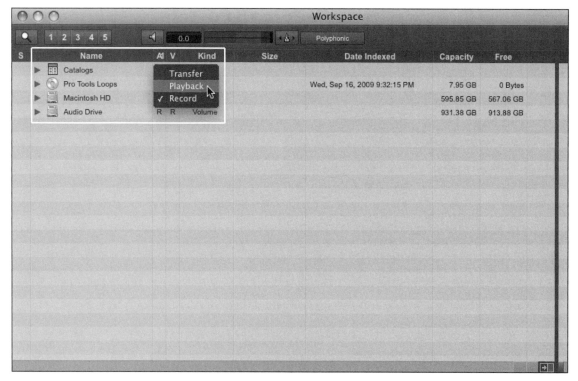

Figure 3.7   Designating a volume as Playback in the Workspace.

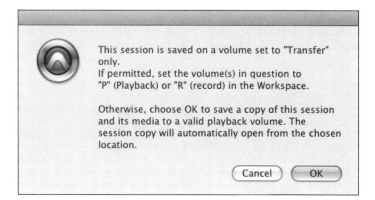

Figure 3.8   Opening a session from a Transfer volume will cause this message to appear.

Pro Tools will automatically assign the Record designation to any hard drive that meets minimum specifications, whereas network, Flash memory, and read-only volumes are always designated as Transfer.

Creating a Click Track

When recording music in Pro Tools, it is always a good idea to use a click track. No only will this help with editing (the click will help keep the recordings close to the grid), but will also help in mixing with time-based effects (such as delay and chorus) because most of them can automatically respond to the session tempo.

Although Pro Tools doesn't have a built-in click system as such, it does have a much more customizable and flexible system. The one potential downside is that it may require a little bit of setup. The degree of setup required depends on the specific characteristics you want the click to have. This section covers the click from the simplest setup and progresses to the most customized.

You can't get any simpler than having Pro Tools create a click when it creates a new session. So let's kick this off by enabling the Automatically Create Click Track in New Sessions preference.

Turning on the preference that allows Pro Tools to create a click track each time a new session is created:

1. Choose Setup > Preferences.

2. In the MIDI tab, click on the Automatically Create Click Track in New Sessions checkbox, shown in Figure 3.9.

3. Of course, if you are in a session that doesn't have a click track, you still need to create one. To do so, you choose Track > Create Click Track, as shown in Figure 3.10.

4. When you select Create Click Track, Pro Tools creates an Aux track, places a plug-in called Click on the first insert, names the track Click, and puts the track in Solo Safe mode (this will allow the click to be heard even if a track is soloed). As you might have guessed, you can swap out the DigiRack Click plug-in for a different one if you prefer (this is discussed a little bit later). At this point, though, the click won't make a sound until Pro Tools broadcasts a click message.

5. While you are enabling the click, you can also enable count off in the Transport window. To do so, you click on the Metronome button in the Transport window (shown in Figure 3.11) or press 7 on the numeric keypad.

6. Click on the Count Off button in the Transport window (shown in Figure 3.12) or press 8 on the numeric keypad to enable the count off.

By default, with Click/Count Off enabled, Pro Tools will generate a click with a 2-bar count off, regardless of whether you are playing or recording. Although this might be fine, if you prefer, you can adjust these defaults in the Click and Countoff Options dialog box.

Setting Pro Tools to click only during record with a 1-bar count off:

1. Double-click the Metronome button in the Transport window to open the Click/Countoff Options dialog box.

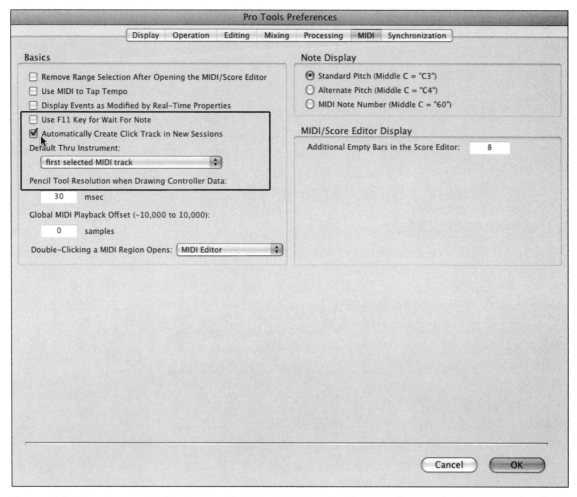

Figure 3.9 The Automatically Create Click Track in New Sessions preference in the MIDI tab of the Preferences dialog box.

2.   Click the Only During Record radio button in the Click section of the dialog box.

3.   Check the Only During Record checkbox in the Count Off section.

4.   Type "1" in the Bars field.

With the settings shown in Figure 3.13, Pro Tools will not click or count off during playback, even though they are both enabled in the Transport window. There will be a click when Pro Tools is recording, but the count off will only be a single bar.

Along with adjusting the Click/Countoff options, you can also change the actual click sound and level of accented and unaccented beats directly from the Click plug-in window.

Figure 3.10 Choosing Create Click Track from the Track menu.

Figure 3.11 The Metronome button in the Transport window.

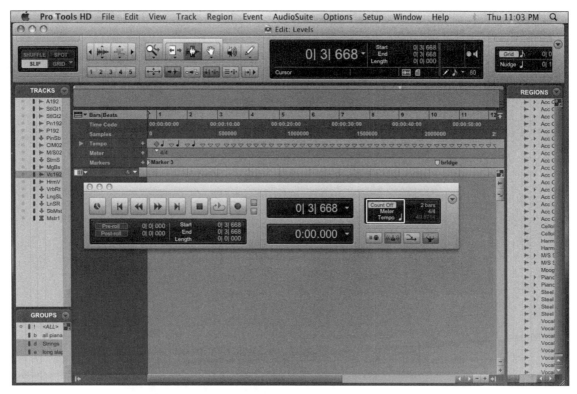

Figure 3.12   The Count Off button in the Transport window.

Figure 3.13   Click/Countoff Options dialog box with the Only During Record settings enabled.

Adjusting the click sound and levels:

1.   Click on the DigiRack Click insert on the click track to open the plug-in window.

2.   Click in the Librarian menu and select the MPC Click preset (shown in Figure 3.14).

3.   Adjust the levels for Accented and Unaccented beats to taste.

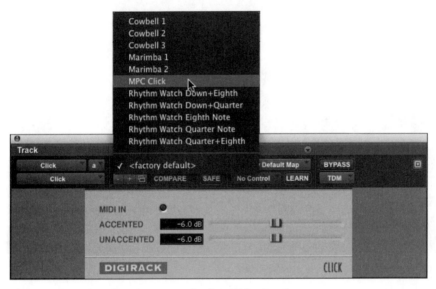

Figure 3.14   The Librarian menu in the Click plug-in.

If you are not happy with any of the available click sounds in the DigiRack Click plug-in, you can swap out the DigiRack plug-in with another click-supported plug-in. TL Metro, for example, has additional click sounds and the ability to add sub-divided beats. If you want to give TL Metro a try, all you have to do is replace the DigiRack Click with TL Metro on the click track.

Changing the DigiRack Click plug-in to TL Metro:

1.   Click on the DigiRack Click insert on the click track to open the plug-in window.

2.   In the RTAS Plug-In selection pop-up menu, choose Plug-in > Instrument > TL Metro, as shown in Figure 3.15.

Last, but not least, if you aren't happy with any of the click plug-in options, you can have Pro Tools send MIDI notes to any virtual or physical MIDI instrument. You can choose the pitch, velocity, and duration independently for both accented and unaccented beats. To illustrate this, let's use the kick and snare of Boom as a click.

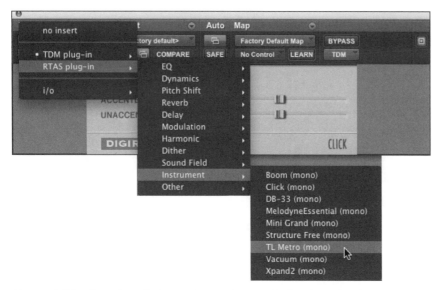

Figure 3.15 Choosing TL Metro from the RTAS Plug-in Selection pop-up menu (shown here with a Pro Tools HD system).

Using the Boom kick and snare as a click:

1. Replace the current click supported plug-in (DigiRack Click or TL Metro) with Boom by choosing RTAS Plug-in > Instrument > Boom on the click track.

   If you have more than one Boom instrument in your session, be sure to take note of the MIDI node that Click Boom is using. This way you can be sure that you are sending the click MIDI events to the correct Boom plug-in. See Figure 3.16.

2. Double-click the Click enable button in the Transport window to open the Click/Countoff Options dialog box.

3. Type "C1" in the Accented Note box and D1 for Unaccented Note.

4. Select your Click Boom plug-in from the Output pull-down window.

   The Output pull-down menu should be set to None when using the DigiRack Click or the TL Metro plug-in.

If your settings match Figure 3.17, you should hear a kick drum for the first beat of the bar, followed by three snare hits when you are recording.

Setting the Input Monitor

When an audio track is record-enabled, you or your system needs to decide whether the track will pass the signal it receives from input to the monitors or will play whatever is on the active track playlist. Most of the time this choice is made intelligently by the system. For instance, if a

Figure 3.16   The MIDI node of this Boom is Boom 2.

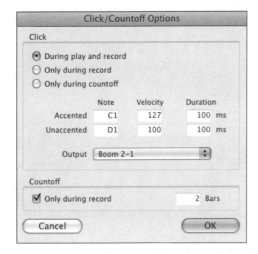

Figure 3.17   Click/Countoff Options dialog box showing MIDI notes C1 and D1 being used for the click.

track is not prepped for recording, Pro Tools will automatically play from the track's active playlist. If the track is currently being recorded to, however, Pro Tools will automatically pass the input audio signal to the monitors.

There is a gray area, however. What should Pro Tools do if a track is record-enabled, but the session is only playing back (meaning the Transport is not set to record)? This is a tough question to answer because it depends on what you are trying to accomplish. At certain times you might want to listen back to what was previously recorded, so you would want the record-enabled tracks to ignore the input signal and play what you see on the track. Other times, however, you might want to practice a part or set recording levels. In this case, you would want Pro Tools to pass the input signal out to the monitors and disregard any audio already on the track.

Not only are both of these common and frequent occurrences, but you may find yourself encountering both of these situations during the same recording session (possibly only moments apart). Fortunately, both these situations are addressed with Pro Tools' two input monitor modes:

- Auto Input Monitoring
- Input Only Monitoring

Input Only Monitoring is relevant only to audio tracks that are record-enabled. Aux Input tracks are always passing signal from their inputs, and audio tracks that are not record-enabled are always reading from disk. So before moving on, be sure you have a session with an audio track that is record-enabled. Also, it might be a good idea to have an audio region on the track to help compare the different input monitor modes.

Here is a quick description of each input monitor mode:

- **Auto Input Monitoring**: The signal path of a record-enabled audio track will automatically switch from the track's input to the track's playlist when the session is playing back. This means that you can quickly hear what you just recorded without having to disarm the track first.
- **Input Only Monitoring**: The signal path will always pass signals from the input as long as the track is record-enabled, regardless of whether the Transport is recording or just playing back.

Generally, Auto Input Monitoring will suit most applications. If you are trying to set levels, practice a performance, or need to punch in to fix a previous pass, however, you may want to switch to Input Only Monitoring.

Changing the input monitor to Input Only Monitoring:

1. Choose Track > Input Only Monitoring, shown in Figure 3.18, or press Opt+K to toggle the Input Monitor status.

When the Input Monitor status is set to Input Only Monitoring, the Input Monitor Status indicator in the Transport window will turn green (see Figure 3.19).

Figure 3.18 Choosing Input Only Monitoring from the Track menu.

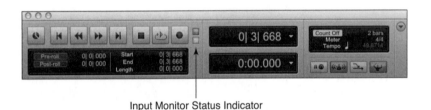

Input Monitor Status Indicator

Figure 3.19 The Transport window shows Input Monitor status.

If you have a microphone or instrument plugged in, you will notice that regardless of whether the Transport is stopped, playing, or recording, the input signal will always pass the signal to the monitors.

Changing the input monitor to Auto Input Monitoring:

1. Choose Track > Auto Input Monitoring, shown in Figure 3.20, or press Opt+K to toggle the Input Monitor status.

Figure 3.20 Choosing Auto Input Monitoring for the Track menu.

Now, if you perform the same experiment as before, you will notice that you can hear the input signal when the Transport is stopped or recording. However, when the Transport window is playing, it will cut off the input signal and play the audio on the track.

This menu option will adjust the input monitor for all record-enabled tracks in the session. If you are working in Pro Tools HD, you can enable input monitoring on a track-by-track basis.

Setting a single track to Input Only Monitoring:

1.   Click on the TrackInput button of the desired track. See Figure 3.21.

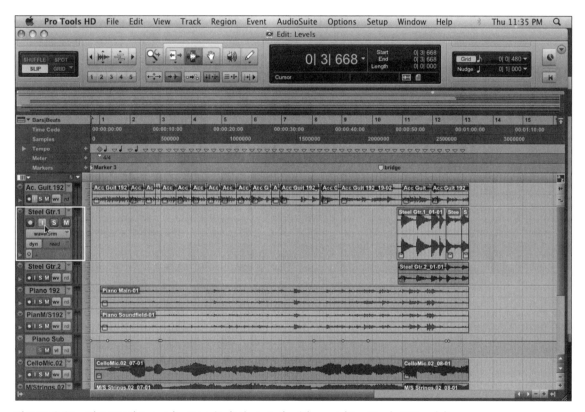

Figure 3.21   The TrackInput button is designated with an I (Pro Tools HD only).

When the TrackInput button is green, that track is in Input Only Monitoring. Otherwise it is in Auto Input Monitoring mode.

Reducing Latency (LE Only)

When you start recording with a Pro Tools LE system, you may notice that there is a delay between when the sound initially occurs and when the sound is actually heard through the monitors. This delay is caused by *latency* and is a factor of working a host-based DAW. Although there is no way to completely eliminate latency from the system, it can be reduced to negligible levels for the purposes of recording (which is where latency is most noticeable).

One way to reduce latency is to reduce the size of the hardware buffer. The hardware buffer, in a sense, is a holding tank for the digital audio in the session. This buffer is required in order to give the CPU adequate time to process the audio before it outputs from your system. If it is too large, the audio is held there for a longer period than it needs to be. As such, there is an added delay that can be problematic when recording. If the buffer is too small, however, there may be artifacts, such as pops and clicks, in your audio and you may even see a DAE –6086 error, as illustrated in Figure 3.22.

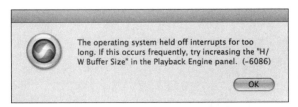

Figure 3.22   DAE –6086 error message.

Which buffer setting gives you the best performance? Well, it really depends on the objective you are trying to achieve. For instance, if you are in the recording stage of a session and there aren't many plug-ins or real-time processes happening, you should be able to set the buffer fairly low before you notice any pops, clicks, or errors.

As your session progresses towards the mixing stages, however, it may become more complex with edits and real-time plug-ins. Thus, you may find that clicks and pops may begin to occur. This is because the host computer needs the extra time to perform all of the calculations required. By increasing the buffer size, you are giving the computer some additional time to process the audio. Because you will usually not be recording/overdubbing while you are mixing, the added latency is much less an issue.

The bottom line is that the hardware buffer size is something you should become comfortable with, because you may find yourself adjusting it often.

Reducing the H/W buffer size to get low latency for recording:

1.   Choose Setup > Playback Engine to open the Playback Engine dialog box, shown in Figure 3.23.

2.   From the H/W Buffer Size pop-up menu, choose the smallest buffer size (measured in samples) possible that allows Pro Tools to play back without pops or clicks. See Figure 3.24.

If you are working with a 002, 003, or Mbox 2 Pro, you can also engage Low Latency Monitoring mode in the hardware setup. When you enable Low Latency Monitoring, Pro Tools

Figure 3.23 Choosing Playback Engine from the Setup menu.

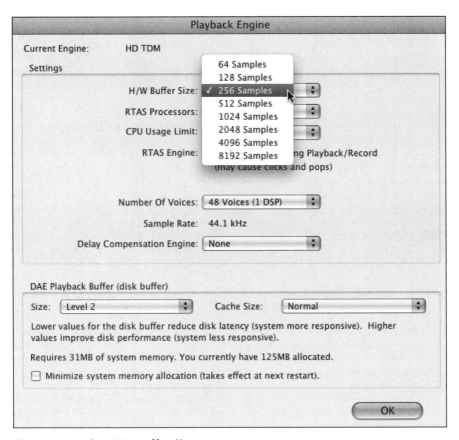

Figure 3.24 The H/W Buffer Size pop-up menu.

optimizes the monitor path to reduce latency as much as possible. Only tracks that are record-enabled and assigned to Outputs 1 and 2 are affected.

Enable Low Latency Monitoring (002, 003, and Mbox 2 Pro only):

1.   Record-enable the desired audio tracks.

2.   Assign the tracks' output to 1–2.

3.   Choose Options > Low Latency Monitoring, as shown in Figure 3.25.

     This option appears only if Pro Tools detects a 002, 003, or Mbox 2 Pro connected to the system.

Figure 3.25   Choosing Low Latency Monitoring from the Options menu.

Although there isn't a software-based low latency option if you happen to be running an Mbox, Mbox 2, or Mbox 2 Mini, there is a way to physically route the input signal directly to the output of the interface. Because the signal doesn't have to enter the computer system, this can be thought of as a "zero latency" solution.

Mbox, Mbox 2, and Mbox 2 Mini each contain a Mix knob. When this knob is pointed straight up at 12 o'clock, it mixes equal amounts of signal directly from the input and any signal that is playing back from your session. As you turn the knob counterclockwise, the amount of signal coming from the session is reduced, thus making the sound coming from the input appear louder. As you turn the knob clockwise from 12 o'clock, the amount of signal directly from the input is reduced, thus making the signal playing back from your session appear louder. So with this knob, you can set the perfect mixture of input and session audio.

Since the interface can hardwire the input to the output, there is no latency in the system. Although the Mix knob can provide you with a nice blend of audio coming from the computer and signal directly from the input, you may find that you hear a doubling of the signal that is coming from the input. This is because the input signal is not only being physically routed directly to the output, but also is routed to the monitors through the record-enabled audio track. In this case, you can eliminate the doubling effect by simply muting the audio track. Because track muting occurs at the track output, the input signal will still record even if the track is muted.

Set up the Mbox for zero latency monitoring:

1. Record-enable and mute the desired track.

2. Adjust the Mix knob to provide the most appropriate mix of input signal and session audio.

3. When recording is complete, return the Mix knob to the 12 o'clock position and unmute the track.

With all of the setup complete, you have actually completed the most complicated part of the recording process.

Tutorial 12: Loop and Punch Recording

In Chapter 2, you learned how to record the audio output of virtual instruments. Rather than focus on standard linear recording here, this section focuses on loop and punch recording. In addition, destructive record is discussed later in this chapter (see "Tutorial 14: Miscellaneous Recording Techniques" for more information).

Loop Recording

Loop recording allows you to define a loop by setting mark-in and mark-out points. While recording, Pro Tools will continue to loop between these points. Each pass creates a separate region, yet all passes are included in a single audio file. Although this may sound like a trivial way to handle each pass, this approach has some advantages, which are discussed in more detail in the "Vamp Recording" section later in this chapter.

Here is the standard workflow when using loop recording:

1. Set the mark-in and mark-out points.

2. Adjust the pre-roll amount.

3. Enable Loop Record.

4. Perform the recording.

5. Select one of the passes as the main take.

So let's get started by marking in and out points.

Setting mark-in and mark-out points for loop recording:

1. Link the Timeline and Edit selections by clicking on the Link Timeline and Edit Selection button, as shown in Figure 3.26.

Figure 3.26 The Link Timeline and Edit Selection button.

2. Do one of the following to create the mark-in and mark-out points:

   a. Drag over the desired area of the track or ruler with the Selector tool, as shown in Figure 3.27.

   b. Press Play in the Transport window. Click the down arrow to set the mark-in point, and click the up arrow to set the mark-out point.

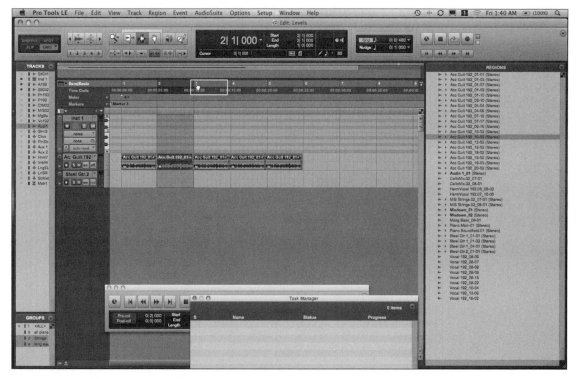

Figure 3.27 Selecting by dragging over the ruler.

On occasion, you may want to hear a bit of the session before the recording begins. You can set the pre-roll amount to be any length—either by typing in a specific time or by simply dragging the pre-roll flag in the ruler.

Adjusting the pre-roll amount:

1. Open the Transport window.

2. Type the desired amount of pre-roll in the Transport window, as shown in Figure 3.28. Or, you can drag the pre/post-roll flags graphically, as shown in Figure 3.29.

3. Press Command+K to enable or disable pre/post-roll.

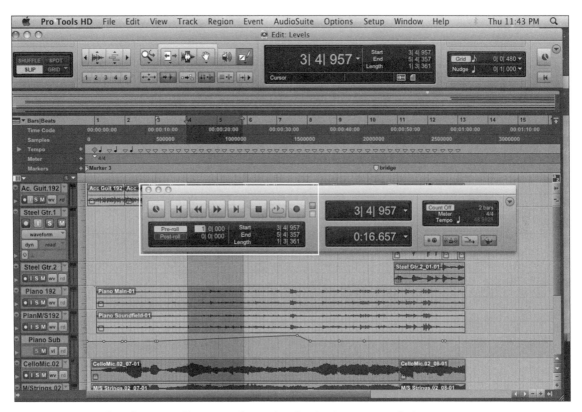

Figure 3.28 Setting the pre-roll amount by typing in the Transport window.

If the Transport window is in standard Record mode (the Record button is shown as a solid red dot), Pro Tools will start playing back at the pre-roll point and then perform a record punch between the mark-in and mark-out points (marked with red up and down arrows), after which time it will stop. To have Pro Tools cycle between the mark-in and mark-out points, you must first enable Loop Record in the Transport window.

Figure 3.29 Setting the pre-roll amount by dragging the flag in the ruler.

Enabling Loop Record:

1. Right-click on the Record button in the Transport window.

2. Choose Loop from the pop-up menu (shown in Figure 3.30).

3. Or press 5 on the numeric keypad to toggle Loop Record on and off.

Figure 3.30 The Record Options pop-up menu can be accessed by right-clicking on the Record button in the Transport window.

Now all you have to do is set the Transport to record and capture the recording. It is important to always stop the Transport in the first half of the loop. Pro Tools will ignore any take that isn't at least half of the total loop. So by stopping the Transport in the first half of the loop, you ensure that the last take captured (which would be the previous take) is the full length of the loop. This is crucial when you want to listen to some of the alternative takes that were recorded.

Loop-recording four passes:

1. Right-click on the Record button in the Transport window.

2. Record-enable the desired track.

3. Press 3 on the numeric keypad to begin recording.

4. Press Stop before the halfway point on the fifth pass, as shown in Figure 3.31.

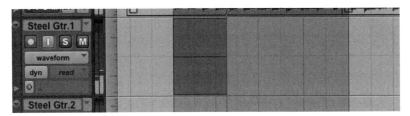

Figure 3.31   It is important to stop the Transport before the halfway point when loop recording.

Even though the fifth pass started, Pro Tools ignored it because it was less than half of the total loop length. As a result, there are only four takes created.

Now you can switch and listen between any of the takes in order to find the best one. (There is a way to make a composite that contains parts of each take in order to make one super take, but I don't cover that issue until the next chapter. Until then, you'll learn how to pick the best complete take of a loop recording session.)

Selecting an alternate take created from the Matches list:

1. With the Grabber, right-click on the newly recorded region.

2. Choose an alternate take from the Matches submenu, as shown in Figure 3.32.

3. If no match is found, choose Matches > Match Criteria. The Matching Criteria window will appear, as shown in Figure 3.33.

4. In the Matching Criteria window, make sure that Track ID and Region Start and End are both checked.

5. Close the Matching Criteria window. Alternate takes should now show up in the Matches submenu.

Vamp Recording

There may be times when you want to record a soloist but don't want to put a specific limit on the overall length of the solo. For instance, you might want to record someone soloing over

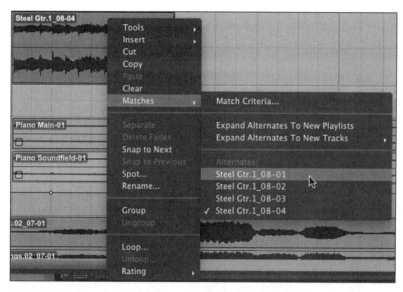

Figure 3.32 The Matches submenu shows the matches to all relevant takes based on the setting of the Matching Criteria window.

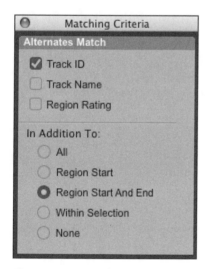

Figure 3.33 The Matching Criteria window.

a jazz standard, and the specific number of choruses that the soloist will take is unknown. Or maybe you want to just brainstorm ideas over a chord progression. In either case, it could be hard to estimate how long the accompanying tracks need to be in order to capture the entire performance.

In these cases, you can use Loop Record to loop over a chord progression infinitely (well, until the disk limit is reached or until you run out of disk space). Although it looks like each pass is a separate file, the reality is that Pro Tools records all takes in one continuous file. As such, after you finish recording, you can select the whole file region, which will contain all of the passes strung together in one continuous solo.

With the whole file region having a specific length, you can then duplicate the accompanying track to the proper length.

Using Loop Record to record a solo of an unknown length:

1. Set up for Loop Record by setting the mark-in and mark-out points, adjusting the pre-roll amount, and so on, as described previously in this chapter.

2. Start recording and allow the soloist to play until she is finished (or until the maximum record time limit is reached).

3. Adjust the match criteria to show matches for Track ID and Region Start.

4. In the Matches list, choose the yellow take, as shown in Figure 3.34.

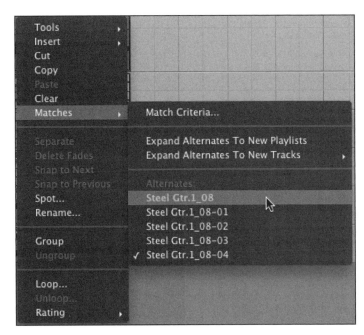

Figure 3.34 The yellow take symbolizes the entire recording, aka the whole-file region.

5. Select the regions on the accompanying tracks.

6. Press Command+D to duplicate the regions on the accompanying tracks to fill the duration of the solo, as shown in Figure 3.35.

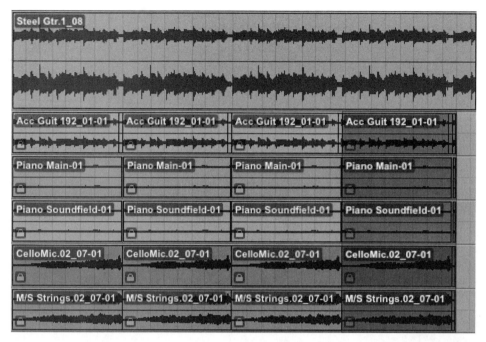

Figure 3.35 Duplicating the accompanying tracks to match the total solo length.

QuickPunch Recording

QuickPunch allows you to punch in and punch out in real-time on a track. To accomplish this, Pro Tools requires an additional disk track voice. So if you maxed out the number of audio tracks, you need to make a couple of audio tracks inactive (see the previous chapter for how to do this) in order to free up enough resources to take advantage of QuickPunch.

QuickPunch is often used in musical contexts where you may want to punch in at multiple points in a track (that is, punching in from bars 6–8 and from bars 17–20). Furthermore, if you have an 002, 003, Control Surface, or ICON Worksurface, you can even control the punch status with a footswitch.

Using QuickPunch recording with a footswitch:

1. Connect a footswitch to your LE interface or control surface.

2. Record-enable the desired track(s).

3. Right-click the Record button in the Transport window.

4. Select QuickPunch from the pop-up menu. A P will appear in the center of the Record button, as shown in Figure 3.36.

5. Press Play in the Transport window.

Figure 3.36 QuickPunch is designated by a P centered in the Record button.

6. Press down on the footswitch every time you want to punch in recording, as shown in Figure 3.37.

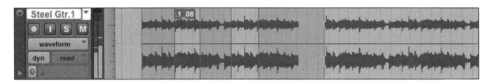

Figure 3.37 QuickPunch recording over multiple sections of a track.

Tutorial 13: Recording MIDI Data

Although the previous chapter talked about entering MIDI notes using the MIDI Event list or by drawing them in the MIDI Editor pane, you can record MIDI with the same traditional recording methods used to record audio. In fact, Pro Tools also has a couple of MIDI-specific recording enhancements that will make it even easier to capture your ideal performance.

Before jumping in and recording, however, you need to set up MIDI Thru.

Setting Up MIDI Thru

Just like setting the Input Monitor mode tells Pro Tools how to handle audio that is coming into its audio inputs, setting the MIDI Thru option tells Pro Tools how to handle MIDI input. If MIDI Thru is set to None, Pro Tools will not pass any MIDI data along unless a MIDI or instrument track is record-enabled. This is useful if you are using a MIDI device that doesn't have the ability to disable local control, such as a Disklavier piano.

Besides no MIDI Thru, there are two other options available in Pro Tools:

- Route MIDI data to the first selected MIDI or instrument track.

- Always route MIDI data to a specific default instrument.

Routing MIDI to the first selected track is a nice, elegant way to handle MIDI data, as it resembles a workflow that is very similar to audio recording. Essentially, you select a track, and as you play your MIDI controller, you hear the sound of that track's instrument.

Some composers, however, like to write on one instrument and then arrange for another instrument at a later time. For instance, many orchestral composers will write with a grand piano and arrange for the orchestra afterward. As such, they may prefer to only hear the Grand Piano virtual instrument, regardless of which track is selected. In either case, setting MIDI Thru is easy.

Setting up MIDI Thru to route MIDI to the top-most track:

1.   Choose > Setup > Preferences and click on the MIDI tab.

2.   Choose Follows First Selected MIDI Track from the Default Thru Instrument pull-down menu, as shown in Figure 3.38.

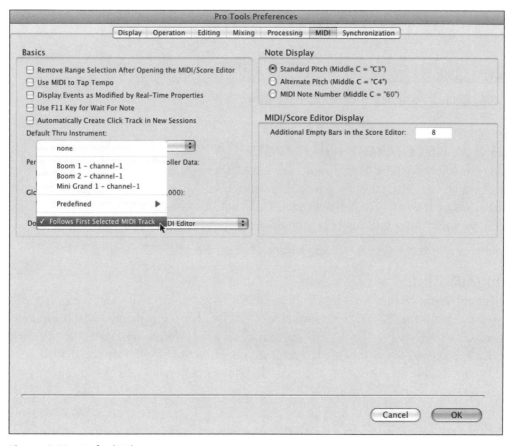

Figure 3.38   Default Thru Instrument pop-up menu.

Pro Tools will pass MIDI data to the selected MIDI track, the top-most selected track (if more than one track is selected), or the MIDI or Instrument track at the top of the session (if no track is selected).

Setting up MIDI Thru to route MIDI to a specific MIDI instrument or channel:

1.   Create an instrument track with the virtual instrument.

2.   Choose Setup > Preferences and click on the MIDI tab.

3.   Choose the desired virtual instrument or MIDI channel under the Default Thru Instrument pull-down menu (shown in Figure 3.39).

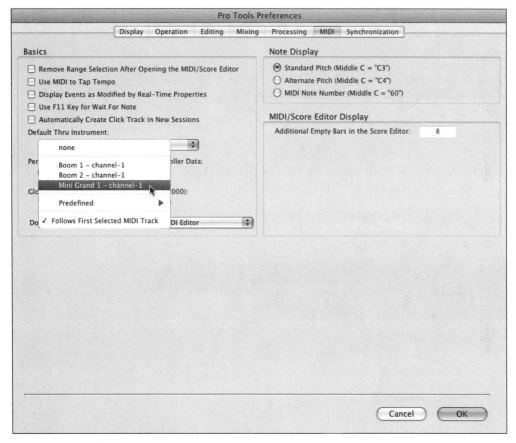

Figure 3.39   Default MIDI Thru set to Mini Grand.

In Figure 3.39, Pro Tools will always route MIDI to Mini Grand, regardless of which track is selected. Once a MIDI or instrument track is record-enabled, however, MIDI Thru is bypassed, and data is passed to the record-enabled track.

Recording with Wait for Note, Loop Playback, and MIDI Merge

You can use Loop Record to record multiple takes of MIDI data, just like loop recording audio. Setting up Loop Record with MIDI is identical to setting it up for audio. In addition, you can switch between alternate takes and take advantage of "vamp" recording.

You may find, however, that in some cases you want Pro Tools to loop between the mark-in and mark-out points but not create a new take each time it cycles through. Instead, you want Pro Tools to just add to the MIDI data that already exists. This is commonly used to create MIDI drum loops. For instance, you can set up your loop points and then record the kick drum. On the following pass, you can add the snare drum, followed by the hi-hats and so on.

In order to take advantage of this workflow, you need to disable Loop Record and enable Loop Playback and MIDI Merge (MIDI Merge cannot be enabled if the Transport is in Loop Record mode).

Before jumping in, let's start by enabling Wait for Note. Wait for Note gives you an infinite count off when the Transport is set to record. Once a MIDI message is received, Pro Tools will instantly begin recording.

Enabling Wait for Note:

1. Make sure the MIDI controls are being displayed in the Transport window. If not, choose View > Transport > MIDI Controls.

2. Click on the Wait for Note button, shown in Figure 3.40.

Figure 3.40 The Wait for Note button.

If you prefer, you can enable F11 on your keyboard to toggle Wait for Note on and off.

Setting up F11 for Wait for Note:

1. On Mac computers, turn off or remap the desktop function keys (for Volume, Brightness, Expose, and so on).

2. In Pro Tools, choose Setup > Preferences and go to the MIDI tab.

3. Click the Use F11 Key for Wait for Note checkbox, as shown in Figure 3.41.

With Wait for Note enabled, you can now record with Loop Playback and MIDI Merge.

Setting up MIDI Merge and enabling Loop Playback:

1. Set the mark-in and mark-out points, as before.

2. Click on the MIDI Merge button in the Transport window to enable it (shown in Figure 3.42). If it is grayed out, make sure that Loop Record is disabled.

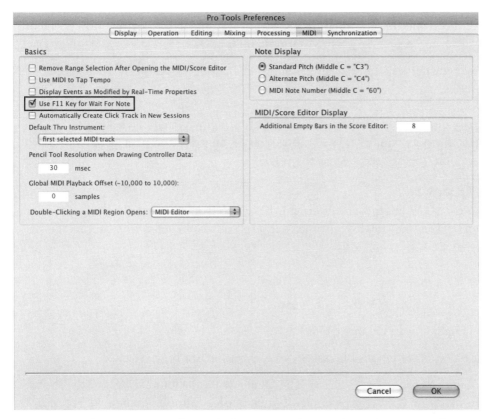

Figure 3.41   The Use F11 Key for Wait for Note preference is on the MIDI Preferences tab.

Figure 3.42   The MIDI Merge button.

3.   Press 4 on the numeric keypad to enable Loop Playback. When Loop Playback is engaged, you will notice a curved arrow in the Play button (shown in Figure 3.43).

Figure 3.43   A curved arrow will appear when Loop Playback is enabled.

4.   Record-enable an instrument track with Boom on it.

5. Click the Record button and then the Play button in the Transport window to record the kick drum for your first pass (MIDI note C1).

6. While the Transport is still recording, add other Boom percussion for each subsequent pass.

You can temporarily disengage recording without interrupting playback by clicking on the Record button in the Transport window. This allows you to hunt for the next percussion sound without having the notes being recorded to the track.

Setting Input Quantize

To help speed up the recording process, you can have Pro Tools automatically quantize the MIDI data on input. This may save you time, because you won't have to quantize the data during the editing phase.

Enabling Input Quantize:

1. Choose Events > Event Operations > Input Quantize.

2. Click the Enable Input Quantize checkbox.

3. Make sure that Note On and Preserve Note Duration are both checked.

4. Set the Quantize Grid to be $\frac{1}{16}$ notes. The Quantize Grid should always be the shortest value you plan to record (for example, if your musical phrase contains $\frac{1}{4}$ notes, $\frac{1}{8}$ notes, and $\frac{1}{16}$ notes, you set the Quantize Grid to $\frac{1}{16}$ notes).

If your Input Quantize settings match Figure 3.44, all recorded MIDI data will be quantized to the nearest $\frac{1}{16}$ note. Although you can close the Event Operations window and still have Input Quantize enabled, it may be wise to leave it open until you're finished using it. That way you can disable and close the window when you are done. Otherwise it can be difficult to know whether it is enabled.

Using Step Input

Another nice feature in Pro Tools is the ability to use your MIDI controller to input MIDI notes without the pressure of having to record them in real-time. With Step Input, you can define the note duration and then press the MIDI note on your controller to determine the pitch. This process allows you to quickly and accurately enter musical phrases, even if they are too difficult to perform in real-time.

Entering a musical phrase with Step Input:

1. Select a track with a Mini Grand virtual instrument (if you don't have one in your session, create one now).

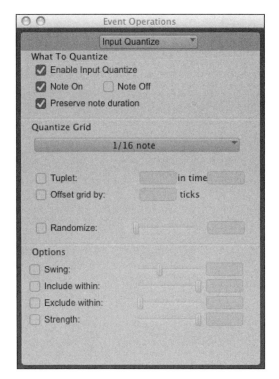

Figure 3.44 The Event Operations window showing the Input Quantize options.

2. Choose Event > Event Operations > Step Input to open the Event Operations window directly to the Step Input options. You can also press Opt+3 on the keypad and choose Step Input from the pull-down menu.

3. Click the Enable checkbox, as shown in Figure 3.45.

4. If the destination track is not the intended track, choose the correct track from the Destination Track pull-down menu.

5. Select a note value.

6. Play a MIDI note on your controller.

You will notice that after you enter the MIDI note, the counter will automatically increment to the next step (determined by the note value). If you play more than one note simultaneously, all the notes will be added to the same step (such as when making a chord).

You can use the keypad to quickly change the note values as you step in your phrase. To take advantage of the numeric keypad shortcuts, however, you must be sure to enable them in the Step Input Event Operations window.

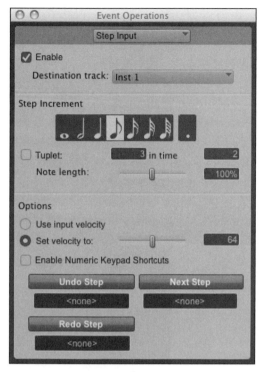

Figure 3.45 The Event Operations window showing the Step Input options.

You need to click the Enable Numeric Keypad Shortcuts checkbox. Here are the Step Input shortcuts for the numeric keypad:

Step Input Shortcuts	Key
Whole note	1
Half note	2
Quarter note	4
Eighth note	5
Sixteenth note	6
Thirty-second note	7
Sixty-forth note	8
Dotted note	. (decimal key)
Toggle tuplet on/off	3
Next step	Enter
Previous step	0

In addition to using the numeric keypad, you can also assign MIDI notes to advance to the next step or undo to a previous step. This is very useful if you have a large MIDI controller keyboard and don't want to constantly take your hands off the keyboard.

In the following example, you'll assign the next step to C8 and the undo step to B7.

Setting up MIDI notes to advance and undo steps:

1.   If the Event Operations window is no longer open, press Opt+3 and select Step Input from the pull-down menu.

2.   Click in the field below the Undo Step button.

3.   Press the B7 key on your MIDI controller.

4.   Click in the field below the Next Step button and press C8 on your MIDI controller.

5.   Press Enter. See Figure 3.46.

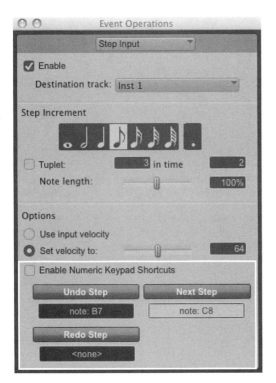

Figure 3.46   MIDI notes set to advance and undo steps.

If your settings match Figure 3.46, as you step input a musical phrase, pressing C8 will add a rest, and pressing B7 will undo the last note entered.

Finally, you should know about the Note Length slider. Normally, the note duration will be the entire duration of the note value. This, however, can be adjusted with the Note Length slider to create more variety in articulation and phrasing. By setting the slider to less or more than 100%, you can create staccato or legato phrases, respectively (see Figure 3.47).

        50% Note Length   100% Note Length   150% Note Length

Figure 3.47   MIDI notes showing note lengths of 50%, 100%, and 150%.

Tutorial 14: Miscellaneous Recording Techniques

In this tutorial, you learn about three recording tricks—one slightly increases the performance of Pro Tools, one shows you how to "create" some shredding guitar solos and recording effects, and one helps you save time by making a two-track bounce.

Using Prime Recording Mode

If you are recording a large number of tracks at the same time (around 20–40 tracks), you might find that it takes Pro Tools a couple of seconds before the Transport starts rolling. By priming the record, you can make Pro Tools use the down time to get ready to record. The result is that Pro Tools will jump into action as you start the Transport!

Setting up Prime Recording mode:

1. Click on the Record button in the Transport window.

2. Right-click on the Play button and select Prime for Record from the pop-up list, as shown in Figure 3.48.

Figure 3.48   Prime for Record can be found by right-clicking on the Play button while the Transport is record-enabled.

Using Half-Speed Recording

Part of the fun of composing is that you never really know where your imagination will take you. Sometimes you will find that you need to record a fast passage but don't have the chops (or don't know someone with the chops) to do it. Well, everyone can be a shredder with half-speed recording! All you have to do is play the passage well at half the required tempo and an octave below the required pitch (required only when recording audio; MIDI data can be played at the regular pitch). If you can't play the phrase an octave down, it may be possible to record at regular pitch and trim the pitch down at a later time. (Elastic Audio and pitch trimming are covered in the next chapter.)

If you plan on playing with a click, it is a good idea to double the speed of the click. That way, when the record happens at half-speed, the click will still sound at its normal rate.

Doubling the speed of the click:

1. Click the Conductor Track button in the Transport window, as shown in Figure 3.49.

Figure 3.49   The Conductor Track button in the lower-right corner of the Transport window.

2. Show the Meter Ruler by choosing View > Rulers > Meter.

3. Double-click on the meter event, as shown in Figure 3.50, to open the Meter Change dialog box.

4. In the Meter Change dialog box, click on the Click pop-up menu and select $\frac{1}{8}$ note, as shown in Figure 3.51.

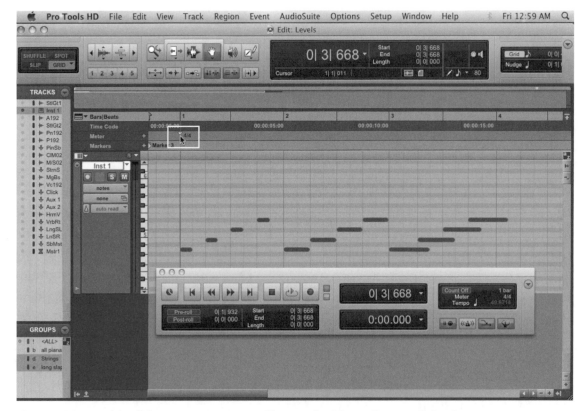

Figure 3.50 Double-click on a meter event will open the Meter Change dialog box.

With the click set up, now all you need to do is record-enable an audio, MIDI, or instrument track and hold down Shift while engaging the Transport!

Do one of the following to record at half-speed:

- Press Shift+3 on the keypad

- Press Shift+Command+Spacebar

Presto! You have instant super-speed shredding without the hours of practice!

Using Destructive Record to "Bounce-As-You-Work"

When most people think about Pro Tools, they relish the idea that they can record over just about anything without losing the previous recording; in other words—*non-destructive recording*. In that light, writing about destructive recording might seem to be a step backward. Destructive recording, however, offers something that goes against the very nature of all non-destructive record modes—the ability to append or replace a portion of an existing audio file.

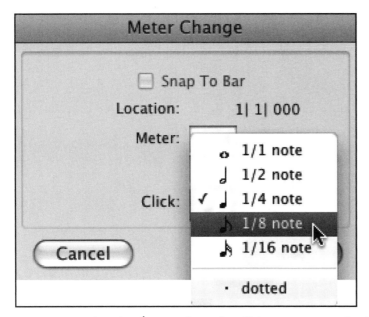

Figure 3.51   Choosing $\frac{1}{8}$ note from the Click pop-up menu in the Meter Change dialog box.

This might not sound like a big deal, but when you consider that Pro Tools doesn't have a real-time bounce, the prospect of appending a long-form project from a midpoint becomes much more appealing.

For instance, let's say that you were contracted to work on a 20-minute film short. After completing the mix, you decided to bounce the session down. About 15 minutes in, you notice a little problem. If the deadline is approaching, that leaves you with a tough choice—let the problem slide or fix the problem and restart the bounce (which will take another 20 minutes to complete). But, maybe there is a third option....

By incorporating destructive record into your workflow, you can simply go back a short period and append to the existing file. This means that if you find a problem at minute 15, you can fix the problem, back up 45 seconds or so, and pick up where you left off.

For this to work, though, you need to route everything that is going to the monitors through an audio track (henceforth referred to as the "mixdown" track) via a bus. If you are on Pro Tools HD, you can set the mixdown track into TrackInput monitor mode and work on your mix (if you're on LE, you will have to put the entire session into Input Only Monitoring and arm the track, which can cause problems if you need to record in other parts of the session).

When you are ready to record, just arm the track, place the Transport into Destructive Record, and let it record your mix. If you need to make an update to your mix, just back up to the last point where the mix was fine and continue recording from there. Destructive Record will append to the existing file. When you are through with the mix, you will find that you have a single file (or stereo pair of files) that contains your entire mix from start to finish.

There is one pitfall that you may need to watch out for. If you are using time-based effects (such as delays or reverb) in your mix, you need to set the pre-roll to be longer than your longest time-based effect.

For instance, if your delay decays over two bars, you should set your pre-roll to be at least two bars. That way, the pre-roll will fill up the delay buffer, and by the time the record drops in, the mix sounds exactly as it would if it had been playing from the start.

Here is a summary of how to set up destructive recording.

Setting up to use Destructive Record while you work:

1. Choose Setup > I/O to access the I/O Setup window; click the Output tab. Rename a bus path "MIX BUS" (refer back to Chapter 1 if you need more information about how to rename an output).

2. Route the outputs of all tracks feeding the monitors to the MIX BUS output, as shown in Figure 3.52.

Figure 3.52 All tracks can be routed from Outputs 1–2 to MIX BUS at the same time by holding the Option key when making the selection from the Track Output Selector pop-up menu.

3. Create an audio track and assign the input to MIX BUS.

4. Set Pro Tools to Input Only Monitoring, or place the Record track in Input Monitor mode (HD only).

5. Record-enable the mixdown track.

6. Set the pre-roll to incorporate the time-based effects.

When you record, stop, and then go backward and record again, you will notice that the region name doesn't change, due to the fact that the file is being appended, as seen in Figure 3.53.

Summary

Well, so ends the recording chapter! There has been a lot of information in this chapter: setup advice that will help your Pro Tools system perform its best even in the most demanding recording session, loop and punch recording tutorials that will allow you to quickly capture the best

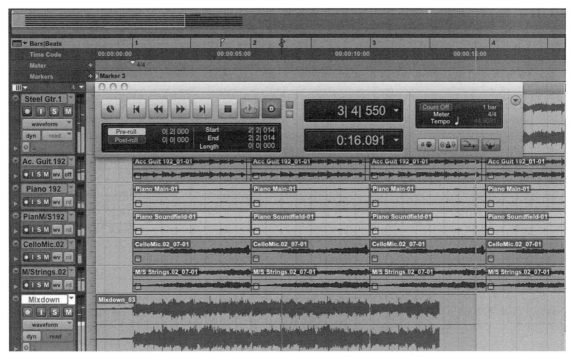

Figure 3.53 Destructive Record appends to the existing file and won't change the filename.

performances, MIDI recording information that will help you create the MIDI performances quickly and accurately, and recording techniques that can't really be categorized, but are good to know when the need arises.

In the next chapter, you will learn many techniques for cleaning up some of these recordings and compositing them into super takes. That is just the beginning of what the next chapter has in store.

4   Editing and Automation

The purpose of this chapter is to illustrate a few common workflows that will increase the quality of your audio while simultaneously decreasing the amount of effort needed to achieve those results.

You will learn how to composite multiple takes, edit MIDI in a variety of ways, take advantage of snapshot automation, and explore some of the AIR plug-ins that come with Pro Tools 8. In addition, the final tutorial introduces a workflow you can use to ensure that you never lose media when you're transferring your session from one computer to another.

Tutorial 15: Compositing Takes in Pro Tools

In Chapter 3, you learned how to use loop recording to create many takes on a timeline selection. You also learned how to switch between each of these takes to find the best one. Here, you are going to take that idea a couple of steps farther with compositing. *Compositing* involves editing together parts of many different sources to create a new whole. For instance, if you find that one take starts off great, but you like the end of a different take, you can stitch them together, thus creating a third take that has the best of both.

Pro Tools has a couple of ways to go about this. The first is the more classic way that is available in most any version of Pro Tools. The second way takes advantage of a new Pro Tools 8 feature—Playlist view—to allow you greater flexibility in compositing.

Because these compositing techniques works well with looped recorded material, you may want to open your loop recording session from Chapter 3. If that session is no longer available, you may want to loop-record something new at this time.

Preparing Your Session

Because you are going to be practicing each of these techniques, it might be a good idea to save your session here. That way if something gets messed up or you just want to try a different method from scratch, you can simply "revert to saved" and get back to the starting point.

With the loop recording completed, it is a good idea to make sure that your session's match criteria are set properly. It shouldn't have changed if you are coming directly from Chapter 3 (Matching Criteria was covered in Tutorial 12), but it never hurts to double-check.

Setting the match criteria:

1.   Right-click on the looped record region and choose Matches > Match Criteria (shown in Figure 4.1) to open the Matching Criteria window.

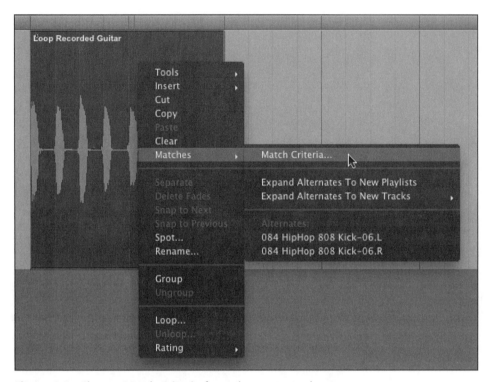

Figure 4.1 Choose Match Criteria from the contextual menu.

2.   Place a check in the Track Name checkbox.

3.   Click the Region Start and End radio button (see Figure 4.2).

Next, you should enable a preference that slightly alters the way the Separate Region command works. This is necessary for the first compositing technique.

Setting the Separate Region preference to help with track compositing:

1.   Choose Setup > Preferences.

2.   Click the Editing tab.

3.   Place a check in the Separate Regions Operates on All Related Takes checkbox (shown in Figure 4.3).

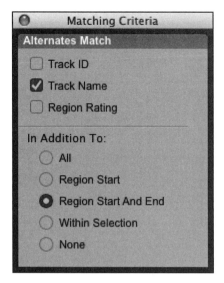

Figure 4.2   Your Matching Criteria window should look like this.

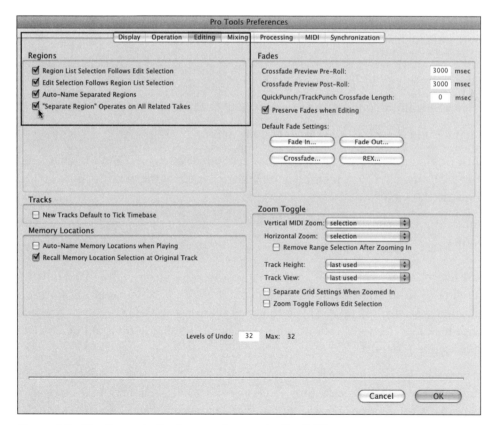

Figure 4.3   The Separate Regions preference in the Editing pane.

With this preference enabled, Pro Tools will cut through all related takes when the Separate Region command is used. Think of it like a stack of pancakes. Each pancake is considered a related take. With the Separate Region Operates on All Related Takes preference enabled, it is like cutting through the entire stack of pancakes, leaving each pancake with an identical set of cuts. Because all of the pancakes are sliced in a similar fashion, you could proceed to swap out the pieces of the bottom pancake with sections of the top pancake if you were so inclined.

Of course, when it comes to pancakes that just seems silly. With audio, on the other hand, it can allow you to create the perfect take by simply swapping out the pieces of the existing take that you don't like.

Compositing with a Single Playlist

Now that you have Pro Tools configured, you can start compositing. As stated earlier, Pro Tools has a couple of ways to go about this. In this first example, you use a single playlist. Essentially, you start by choosing the take that most closely resembles the final. Then, you select and separate the trouble areas. Lastly, you swap out the trouble regions with regions from other takes.

Compositing a track in Waveform view:

1. Right-click on the loop recorded region and choose the best take from the Matches submenu (see Figure 4.4).

2. Highlight a trouble area in that take (see Figure 4.5).

3. Choose Edit > Separate Region > At Selection (or press Command+E) to separate the region.

4. Repeat Steps 2 and 3 for any additional trouble areas.

5. Right-click on the trouble regions and choose a different take from the Matches submenu. Note: The matches shown in this submenu are based on the options chosen in the Matching Criteria window.

6. Use the Smart tool to trim and fade so the transition between the regions is smooth (see Figure 4.6).

Although compositing in a single playlist is useful (especially when using older Pro Tools LE systems), it is not without some faults. First off, it can be difficult to make an appropriate selection because you can only see the top take. This means that there is a certain amount of trial and error involved with making selections, followed by extensive trimming and fading in order to make all of the pieces jibe properly.

It is possible to composite by copying each take to a separate track and then copying sections from each of the tracks onto a new track, thus foregoing the whole matching takes scenario. This workflow can take a toll on your track count and be inconvenient to work with on older Pro Tools LE systems (due to the limited number of tracks).

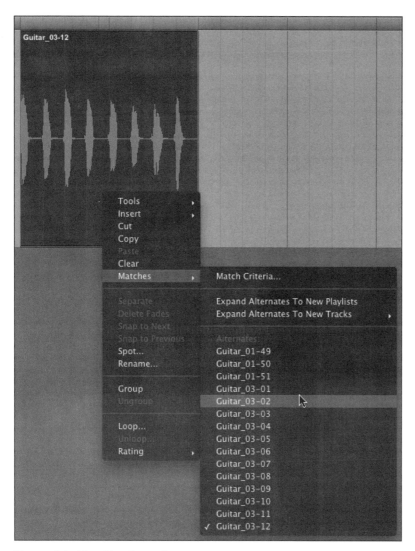

Figure 4.4   The Matches submenu.

Compositing with Playlist View

Pro Tools 8 resolves many of these problems with an entirely new way to composite. This all stems from a new track view in the Edit window called Playlist view. Essentially, it is now possible to have Pro Tools place each take onto a separate playlist and then have them all displayed simultaneously. Because only one playlist can play at a time, you have the advantage of seeing all takes without the problem of losing your track count.

Let's see this in practice. If you need to, it might be a good idea to return your loop-recording region back to its original state (either by undoing your work or by using the File > Revert to Saved command).

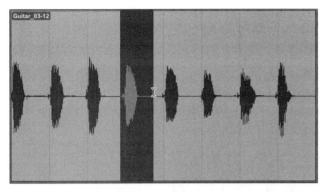

Figure 4.5 Select the "problem" areas of the take.

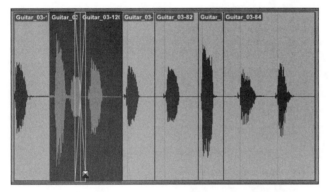

Figure 4.6 Using the Smart tool to create a crossfade.

Expanding and organizing takes in Playlist view:

1. Right-click on the loop-recorded region and choose the best take from the Matches submenu.

2. Right-click on the loop recorded region, and choose Matches > Expand Alternates to New Playlists (shown in Figure 4.7).

3. Choose Playlists from the Track View selector (shown in Figure 4.8).

Now, your loop-recorded track should look something like Figure 4.9, which means you are ready to begin compositing.

Compositing the new take:

1. Select a trouble area.

2. Use the Playlist Solo button to compare different tracks (see Figure 4.10).

3. With command Focus enabled, use P and ; (semicolon) to move the selection up or down (respectively) to the appropriate playlist.

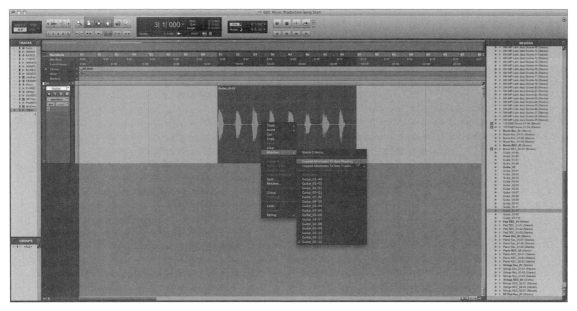

Figure 4.7 Expand Alternates to New Playlists.

Figure 4.8 Choose Playlists from the Track View selector.

4. Adjust the selection to create the smoothest edit.

5. Click the Copy Selection to Main Playlist button (it is the upward-pointing arrow next to the Playlist Solo button) to place the selected content on the main playlist.

6. Repeat for each trouble area.

7. Trim and crossfade as necessary.

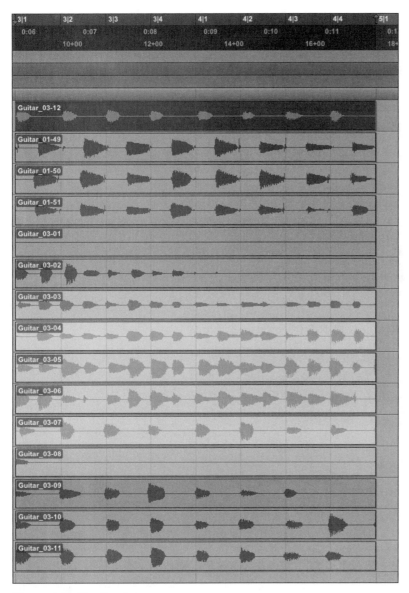

Figure 4.9 Playlist view.

Figure 4.10 Playlist Solo button.

In no time, you can have a composited playlist. Plus, with the playlist color-coding, it is possible to determine which takes were used in the final composite.

Tutorial 16: MIDI Event Editing

In this tutorial, you edit the Vac Bass track (the only MIDI-based track that wasn't recorded down at the end of Chapter 2) using some of Pro Tools' vast array of MIDI editing tools.

Most of Pro Tools' MIDI editing features are localized in the Event menu, more specifically, within the Event Operations submenu. Here you will find an assortment of common MIDI editing operations that will automate some of the more tedious tasks associated with MIDI editing (such as changing timing, duration, pitch, and so on).

Let's start off by enabling Mirrored MIDI Editing. This will allow any changes that are made to one MIDI region to be automatically made to all other identical MIDI regions. Since the Vac Bass track consists of one 2-bar looped region for the majority of the song, any changes that are made in the first iteration of the loop will be reflected throughout the song.

To enable Mirrored MIDI Editing, you simply click on the Mirrored MIDI Editing button, located in the Edit window (shown in Figure 4.11).

Figure 4.11   The Mirrored MIDI Editing button.

Next, you should flatten and looped regions on the Vac Bass track. Although using region loops can really speed up the arrangement process, they can often create unpredictable results when event operations are applied to them.

Flattening all looped regions on the Vac Bass track:

1.   With the Selector tool, triple-click on any region on the Vac Bass track. This will select all its regions, as shown in Figure 4.12.

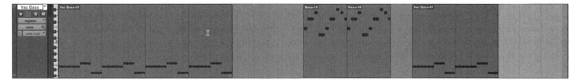

Figure 4.12   Triple-click with the Selector tool to highlight all regions on a track.

2.   Choose Region > Unloop to unloop all looped regions (shown in Figure 4.13).

3.   Click the Flatten button in the dialog box shown in Figure 4.14.

Figure 4.13 The Unloop command can be found on the Region menu.

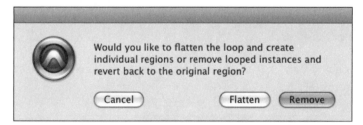

Figure 4.14 The Unloop Region confirmation dialog box.

As an alternative, you can just press Command+Option+U. This key command is technically used to ungroup regions. Since Pro Tools views looped and grouped regions in a similar fashion, however, ungrouping a looped region produces the same result as flattening region loops with the Unloop command from the Region menu (except you don't get the dialog box asking if you would rather flatten or remove the looped instances).

Now you are ready to perform some quick edits to the MIDI performance data on the Vac Bass track. To start, it might be fun to make the Vac Bass more staccato (shorten the duration of the notes). This can cause it to pop out more in the mix.

Modifying MIDI Data with Event Operations

Although you can manually edit each note to be half of its current duration, it is much faster to use the Change Duration operation. This way, you only have to make your selection and run the operation once rather than having to repeat a process over and over again for each individual note.

Shortening the Notes

Shortening all of the Vac Bass notes to be $\frac{1}{32}$ notes instead of $\frac{1}{16}$ notes:

1. Select the first region on the track.

2. Choose Event > Event Operations > Event Operations Window (shown in Figure 4.15) or press Option+3 on your numeric keypad to show the Event Operations window.

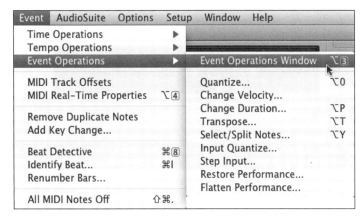

Figure 4.15   Choose Event Operations from the Event menu.

3. Select Change Duration from the pop-up menu at the top of the window (shown in Figure 4.16).

4. In the Set All To field, type "0 | 120."

5. If your Event Operations window looks like Figure 4.17, click Apply.

At this point, you should notice that MIDI notes for the selected region have been shortened to 120 ticks, otherwise known as $\frac{1}{32}$ note (see Figures 4.18 and 4.19 for a before and after comparison). Furthermore, because MIDI Merge was enabled, every other occurrence of that region has also been affected. If it were disabled when you applied the Change Duration operation, Pro Tools would have only processed the selected MIDI notes.

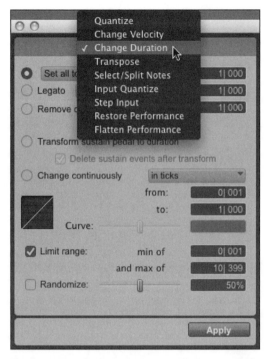

Figure 4.16   There are many event operations available.

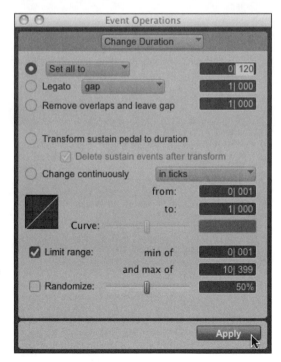

Figure 4.17   The Event Operations window (showing Change Duration).

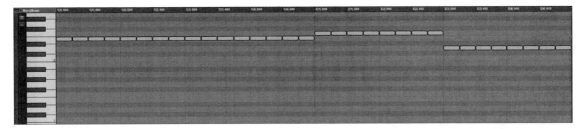

Figure 4.18   Vac Bass MIDI notes, before Change Duration.

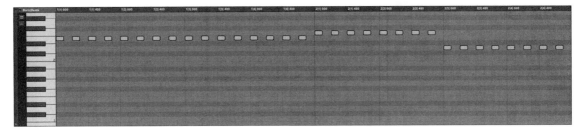

Figure 4.19   Vac Bass MIDI notes, after Change Duration.

Changing the Velocities

Another useful operation to perform on MIDI tracks is Change Velocity. *Velocity* is the speed at which a note is pressed (note-on velocity) or released (note-off velocity). According to the standard MIDI specification, every MIDI note message contains a note-on velocity. In general, when keys are played softly, they are pressed slower than when they are played loudly. As a result, many synthesizer patch designers use velocity to represent performance dynamics (that is, lower velocities create softer tones, whereas higher velocities create louder ones).

You can use this to your advantage by randomizing the velocities in order to make the Bass track more dynamic.

Randomizing the velocities of the Vac Bass track:

1. Open the Event Operations window.

2. Select Change Velocity from the pop-up menu at the top of the window (shown in Figure 4.20).

3. Place a check in the Note On checkbox.

4. Select the Set All To radio button and set the value to 64.

5. Click the Randomize box and set the value to 60.

6. If your Event Operations window looks like Figure 4.21, click Apply.

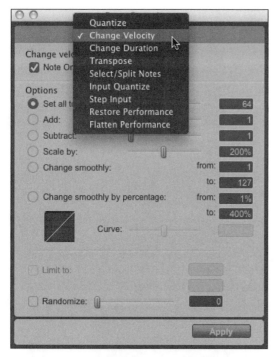

Figure 4.20 Selecting Change Velocity in the Event Operations window.

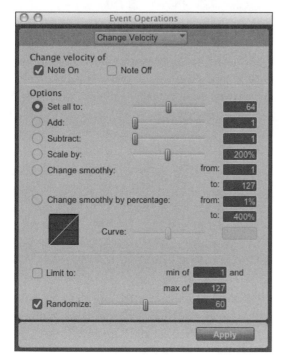

Figure 4.21 The Event Operations window (showing Change Velocity).

In order to see the change, you need to show the Velocity lane below the Vac Bass track by clicking on the Show/Hide automation lanes disclosure triangle (shown in Figure 4.22). Check out Figures 4.23 and 4.24 for a before and after comparison of the Change Velocity operation.

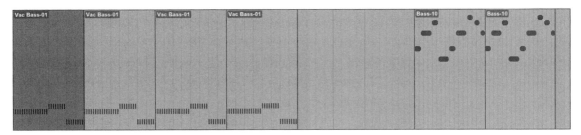

Figure 4.22 The Show/Hide automation lanes disclosure triangle.

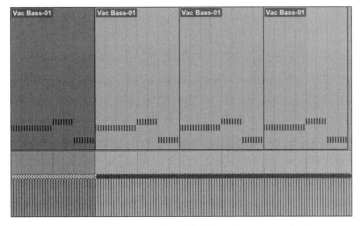

Figure 4.23 Velocity MIDI data, before Change Velocity.

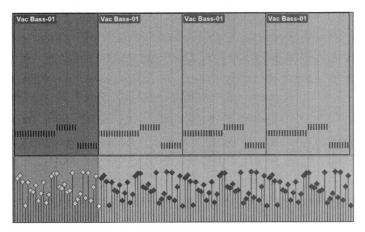

Figure 4.24 Velocity MIDI data, after Change Velocity.

Manually Adding Velocity Sensitivity

At this point you may be wondering why your changes aren't having a drastic effect on the sound quality. This is because the patch you are using emulates a Juno-106. This particular synthesizer didn't respond to changes in velocity, thus this patch wasn't designed to respond to velocity. Just because the original didn't respond to velocity, however, doesn't mean that you can't edit the patch and add it yourself. Furthermore, by adding it yourself, you can adjust how much impact you want the velocity to have over the sound.

Adding velocity sensitivity to the Vac Bass instrument:

1.   Show the Vac Bass Vacuum plug-in.

2.   In the Env One and Env Two sections, turn the VEL knobs until the appropriate amount of velocity control is obtained (shown in Figure 4.25).

Figure 4.25   Envelopes 1 and 2 in the Vacuum plug-in.

Envelope 1 (Env One) will control how much of a filter change velocity has over the patch, whereas envelope 2 (Env Two) will control the amount of amplitude change. In addition to adjusting the VEL knobs, you may want to play around the LPF's (low-pass filter) CUTOFF and RESO knobs to further hear Env One's effect on the patch.

Using the Restore and Flatten Performance Operations

Now that you have made some changes to the MIDI data on the Vac Bass track, it is a good time to talk about the Restore and Flatten Performance operations. Although Pro Tools gives you a great deal of editing power, it also has some flexibility in allowing you to restore one or more aspects of the MIDI performance back to the original recording if you find that you have strayed too far off of the path. In a way, it is like having a second, non-chronological, undo queue that is specific for MIDI data.

There are a couple of restrictions that you should be aware of, though. First, you can only restore performances that were modified with the Event Operations window—any changes made with the Edit tools are instantly locked in (although you can still use the standard Undo to reverse any tool-based changes). Second, any time you use the Flatten Performance operation, you effectively tell Pro Tools that this is the new restore point. As such, you will no longer be able to restore the performance to its original recording (Restore will take you back to the last time you flattened).

To illustrate the use of Restore Performance, you will now restore the duration of the notes on the Vac Bass track.

Using the Restore Performance operation to restore the duration:

1. Select the first region on the Vac Bass track by clicking on it with the Grabber tool.

2. Choose Restore Performance from the pop-up menu at the top of the Event Operations window.

3. Place a check in the Duration checkbox and leave all other boxes unchecked.

4. If your Event Operations window looks like Figure 4.26, click Apply.

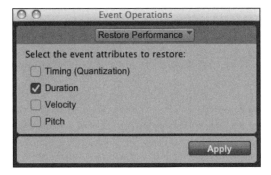

Figure 4.26 The Event Operations window (showing Restore Performance).

You should notice that durations have been restored, but the velocities have been unaffected, even though they were modified after the duration was changed. Because this tutorial actually requires the note duration to be shorter, you should undo the Restore Performance operation (use Command+Z) to bring the bassline back to $^1\!/_{32}$ notes.

Next, you can create a new restore point by using the Flatten Performance operation. When you flatten a performance, you are telling Pro Tools that you are happy with all that processing done to this point. If you decide to restore at some point in the future, you will be restoring back to the last point you flattened. Just like the Restore Performance, you may elect to flatten only specific note attributes, such as note duration or timing.

For the purposes of this tutorial, you will flatten all of the note attributes for the Vac Bass track.

Flattening the MIDI data on the Vac Bass track:

1. With the Selector tool, triple-click on any region on the Vac Bass track to select all regions.

2. Choose Flatten Performance from the pop-up menu at the top of the Event Operations window.

3. Place a check in all the boxes.

4. If your Event Operations window looks like Figure 4.27, click Apply.

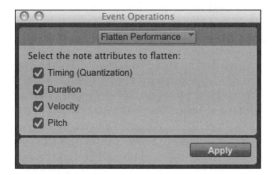

Figure 4.27 The Event Operations window (showing Flatten Performance).

Modifying MIDI Data in the MIDI Editor Pane

Next, you can create some more interest in the bassline by editing the data directly in the MIDI Editor pane. When editing MIDI data, you'll use the Pencil tool. It is sort of a "super" Smart tool because it allows you to perform many editing functions without the need to switch tools. In Chapter 2, you used the Line Pencil tool to create a series of notes based on the custom note duration that all had the same velocity. Here is a brief list of some additional MIDI editing functions that can be performed with the Pencil tool:

- Add, copy, and delete notes

- Separate notes

- Consolidate notes

- Trim note duration

- Trim note velocity

Here you will use the Pencil tool to edit the Vac Bass track in order to make it more interesting.

Adding a $\frac{1}{32}$ note to the bass pattern:

1. Select the first region on the Vac Bass track.

2. Reveal the MIDI Editor pane by choosing View > Other Displays > MIDI Editor, or click on the MIDI Editor Show/Hide icon in the lower-left portion of the track display (shown in Figure 4.28).

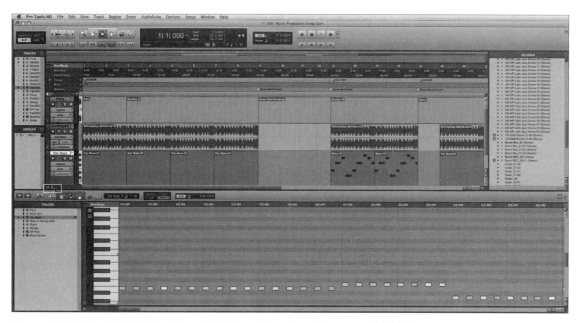

Figure 4.28 The MIDI Editor Show/Hide icon (see boxed area on left side).

3. Click the Grid Value selector in the MIDI Editor pane and set it to $\frac{1}{32}$ note (shown in Figure 4.29).

4. With the Pencil tool, click in the space at 1 | 3 | 120 (shown in Figure 4.30).

5. Command+click and drag up or down on the newly added note to adjust its velocity.

Figure 4.29 Setting the Grid value in the MIDI Editor pane.

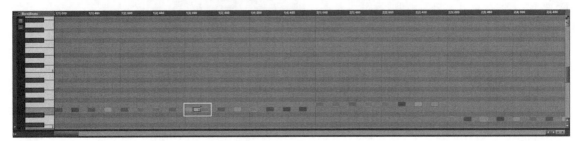

Figure 4.30 Adding a $\frac{1}{32}$ note to the Vac Bass track.

Consolidating two notes to make a single note:

1. Press Control+Shift and hover the cursor over the end of the note at 2 | 3 | 000. The cursor will change to the Consolidate cursor shown in Figure 4.31.

2. Click to consolidate this note with the following note.

3. Command+click and drag on the newly created note to adjust its velocity.

To disable Mirrored MIDI Editing, you simply click on the Mirrored MIDI Editing Enable/ Disable button. With Mirrored MIDI Editing disabled, any changes you make to the bassline

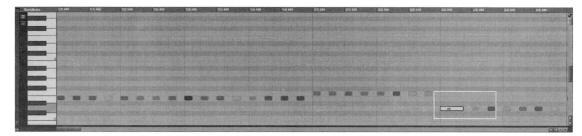

Figure 4.31 Control+Shift+click on a note to consolidate it with the following note.

will only affect the instance that you edited. This is a good time to experiment with the Pencil tool and add some changes to bassline in order to make it sound less repetitious.

Modifying MIDI Data with Real-Time Properties

There is one other interesting way to manipulate MIDI data, and that is through the use of real-time MIDI properties. These properties act like MIDI plug-ins in that they make real-time adjustments to your MIDI data in a non-destructive way.

There are five main properties that you can control:

- Quantizing

- Duration

- Delay

- Velocity

- Transpose

Before jumping in, however, it is a good idea to make sure that Pro Tools will display the effects of the real-time properties on the track data. Otherwise, Pro Tools may change the data in real-time but will only show the original MIDI performance. This setting can be found in the Preferences dialog box.

Setting Pro Tools to display the effects of real-time properties:

1. Choose Setup > Preferences.

2. Click the MIDI tab (shown in Figure 4.32).

3. Place a check in the Display Events as Modified by Real-Time Properties (shown in Figure 4.33).

4. Click OK.

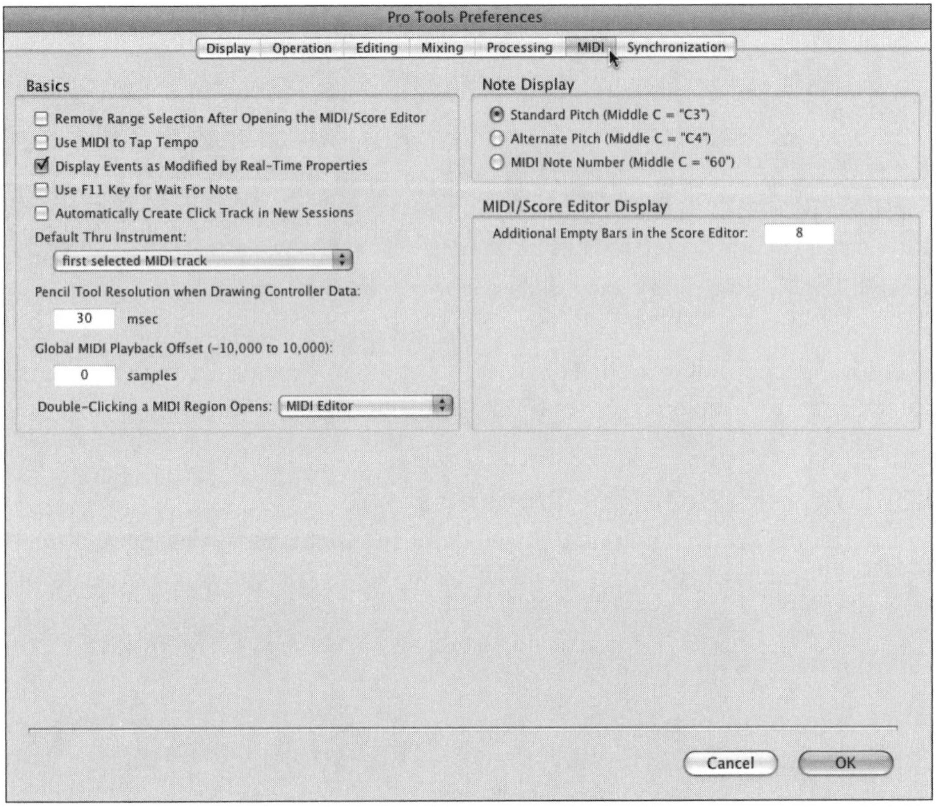

Figure 4.32 The MIDI tab in the Preferences dialog box.

To see how these properties work, let's transpose the Vac Bass track to see if you like it playing in other octave registers.

Transposing the Vac Bass track with real-time MIDI properties:

1. Show the real-time MIDI properties by clicking on the Edit Window View selector (shown in Figure 4.34) and choosing Real-Time Properties (see Figure 4.35).

2. With the Vac Bass track height set to Medium or larger, click on the TRN button to activate the real-time Transpose property (shown in Figure 4.36).

3. In the Oct field, click and drag up to +1 octave for the Bass track.

You should notice a T in the upper-right corner of each region on the Vac Bass track (shown in Figure 4.37). This lets you know that these regions are affected by track-based real-time properties.

When transposing an entire track, it is common to find that the settings may transpose a couple of regions a little too high or too low. In these cases, you can override the track's real-time properties with region-based real-time settings.

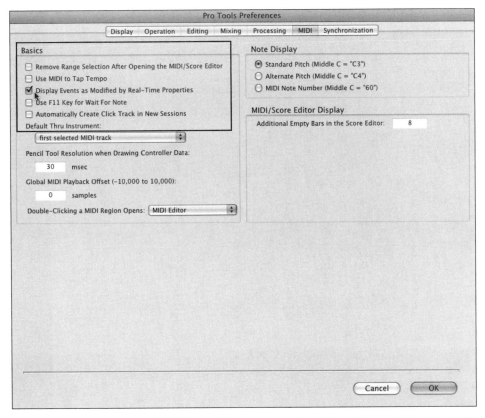

Figure 4.33 Changes applied by real-time properties will not be reflected in MIDI and instrument tracks unless this preference is checked.

To illustration this, let's transpose the bassline in the outro back down to 0 with a region-based real-time property.

Transposing the outro down to 0 octave:

1. Select the last two regions on the Vac Bass track.

2. Choose Event > MIDI Real-Time Properties or Press Option+4 on the numeric keypad to open the Real-Time Properties window.

3. Click the Transpose button.

4. Click and drag down in the Oct field until it is 0.

You should now see an R in the upper-right corner of the selected regions (shown in Figure 4.38). This is to show that these regions are not responding to the track-based settings but rather have their own custom, region-based settings.

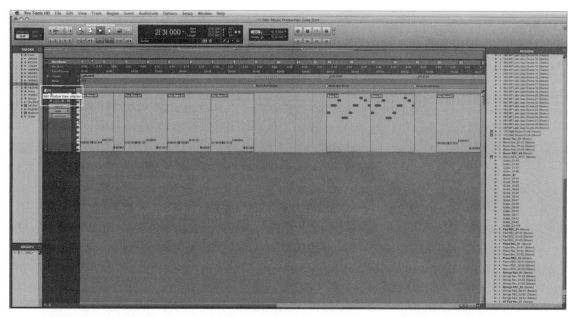

Figure 4.34   The Edit Window View selector.

Figure 4.35   The Edit Window View menu.

If you created a bassline for Section B, now might be a good time to adjust the transposition, if needed. You may also want to experiment with the duration and velocity real-time properties in order to get an idea of how they change the data that is already on the track.

Figure 4.36 Enabling the Transpose real-time property.

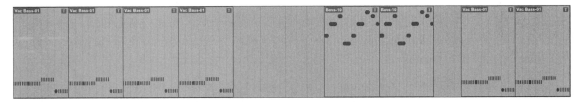

Figure 4.37 A T appears anytime a real-time property is enabled.

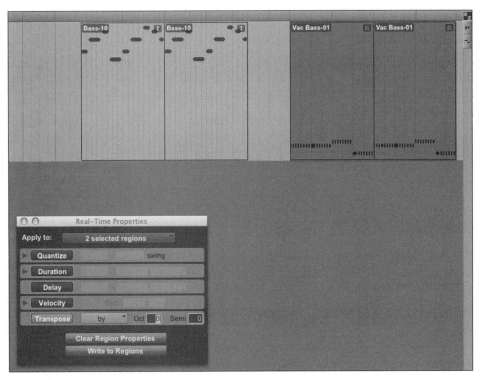

Figure 4.38 An R will replace the T to show that the region's real-time properties are overriding the track's settings.

Tutorial 17: Conforming Grooves with Elastic Audio

In this tutorial, you learn how to tighten the feel between all of the individual tracks in your session through quantizing and conforming.

Quantizing versus Conforming

Quantizing is correcting the timing of a track's events to be closer to a predetermined grid.

Whether reading it from a sheet of paper, playing it to your friend in the garage band, or creating it on a computer, music is always organized on a grid of bars and beats. Music students just starting out tend to read sheet music very literally, and as a result, they tend to play the music in a very sterile manner. As music students develop into professional musicians, they learn to interpret the sheet music based on the performance notes and the musical style of the composition.

Computers tend to read music in a very literal fashion as well. If left to its own devices, a computer will "correct" (or quantize) a recording to such a degree that it will be perfectly in time but will lose much of the intent and style of the original performance, potentially making it sound like a performance of a music student just learning an instrument.

Of course, some music styles, like many types of electronic music or anything from the early to mid-80s that was made with a drum machine, work well with a heavily quantized sound. If you are making music outside of those particular styles, you may find that you need a different approach—one that's groove conforming.

Groove conforming is taking the style of a particular performance and infusing it with audio events in your session. This approach gives all of the tracks, regardless if they were derived from samples, different recording sessions, step inputted MIDI tracks, or idea-generating vamp recordings, a tightened feel with a unity of purpose.

For instance, if you try to identify the tempo of an early Motown recording, you might find that the tempo starts at one speed and changes wildly by the end. So how can a recording that is so "imperfect" (in terms of tempo) feel so right when played? Well, for starters, all of the musicians had the same idea how the music should sound, and they all played their parts to achieve that end. That unity of purpose comes through in the song. In short, it is far more important that all of your tracks appear to have the same unity of purpose than to make sure they are tightly quantized to an evenly spaced grid.

That is not to say that the grid isn't vital in working with Pro Tools; that is like saying that organizing music into bars and beats isn't important. There are times, however, when the style of music dictates that events should be pushed ahead or behind the grid lines in order to preserve the feel of the music.

Quantizing Events

Pro Tools 8 can quantize and conform three types of track events—MIDI notes, audio region start times, and Elastic Audio event markers. In this section, you will quantize the 084 MP Distorted

Drums region from Chapter 2. You may remember that all of the time compressing and expanding made the distorted drums loop a little loose in regards to timing. Fortunately, through the magic of Elastic Audio and quantizing, you can actually correct the timing of this loop, effortlessly.

Quantizing the distorted drums loop to the grid:

1. Triple-click with the Selector tool to select all of the distorted drums regions.

2. Press Option+3 to show the Event Operations window.

3. Choose Quantize from the pull-down menu.

4. Select $\frac{1}{16}$ note from the Quantize Grid menu.

5. Check the Strength checkbox and set its value to 100%.

6. If your window looks like Figure 4.39, click Apply.

Presto! If you compare Figure 4.40 and Figure 4.41, you will notice that the analysis markers have been shifted to the nearest $\frac{1}{16}$ note. The result is that the loop now sounds more tightly connected with the rest of the music.

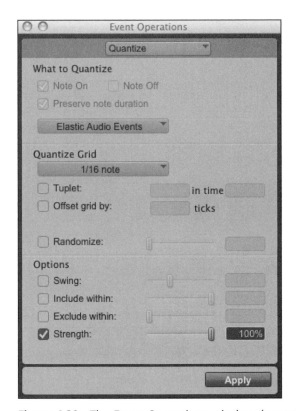

Figure 4.39   The Event Operations window (quantizing an Elastic Audio event).

Notice that the analysis markers don't line up with the grid mark

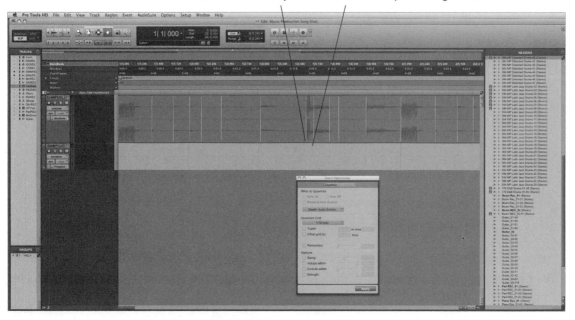

Figure 4.40   Track showing elastic analysis markers before quantizing.

Now they are aligned

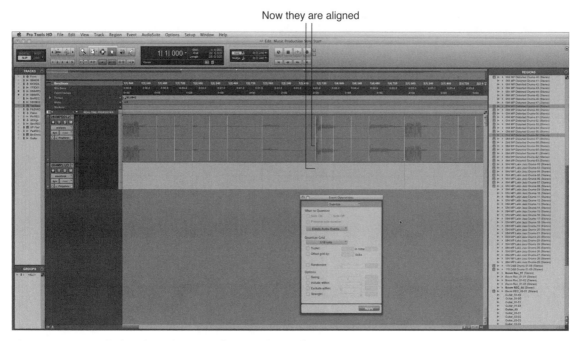

Figure 4.41   Track showing elastic analysis markers after quantizing.

Standard grid quantizing works very well for music that originates on the computer. However, you might find that grid-quantized audio and MIDI will still clash with certain styles of music or specific recorded performances. Although you could mess around with many of the Quantize settings (such as Swing, Strength, Include, and Exclude Within), more often than not it is easier to just use groove quantize. To be even more specific, the best results come from you extracting the groove from a performance that exists in your session and then using that groove to conform the rest of the tracks.

Creating a Groove Template Using Beat Detective

There are a few ways to use groove quantize. One way, for instance, is to apply a predefined groove template to your entire session. This will infuse each track in your session with the feel provided by the template. Pro Tools includes templates based on the feel of other hardware and software programs, such as the MPC, Logic, and Cubase styles.

Pro Tools also gives you the option, through Beat Detective, to analyze and extract a groove template from any audio or MIDI recording. This is a very powerful feature and can be used to tighten your entire session to the region that you believe best encapsulates the feel you are looking for.

In order to take advantage of such a powerful feature, you first need to be familiar with Beat Detective. Beat Detective contains five modes of operation that can process audio and MIDI (well, only the first two modes work with MIDI). Because this tutorial is focused on creating groove templates, only Groove Template Extraction is discussed here; feel free to refer to your reference guide for more information regarding the other modes.

The Beat Detective window (shown in Figure 4.42) is broken into four main areas. The first two areas, Operation and Selection, are always the same. The other two areas will change, depending on the mode of operation. The right-most area contains detailed settings based on the operation mode, and the bottom area is always some sort of "apply" function. In general, you work through this window in a clockwise fashion; you select the operation (in this case Groove Template Extraction), confirm the timeline selection (it should match the bars and beats displayed in the main counter of the Edit window), adjust the transient detection (if Groove Template Extraction is the current operational mode), and finally click Extract (again, assuming that Groove Template Extraction is the current operational mode).

Figure 4.42 The Beat Detective window.

Flattening Region Loops

Let's illustrate the Beat Detective by tightening the intro and Section A to the 084 Hip Hop Kick region to prevent any odd editing mishaps.

Flattening the region loops on the 084 Hip Hop Kick loop track:

1. Triple-click on the Kick track with the Selector tool.

2. Choose Region > Unloop.

3. Click the Flatten button.

Creating a Groove Template

Creating a groove template from the 084 Hip Hop Kick loop:

1. With the Grabber tool, select the first two bars in the 084 Hip Hop Kick region (shown in Figure 4.43).

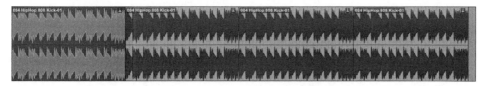

Figure 4.43   The first two bars of the Kick track are selected.

2. Press Command+8 on the numeric keypad to open the Beat Detective window. You can also open it by choosing Event > Beat Detective (shown in Figure 4.44).

3. Choose Groove Template Extraction from the Operation section of the Beat Detective window (shown in Figure 4.45).

Figure 4.44   Selecting Beat Detective from the Event menu opens the Beat Detective window.

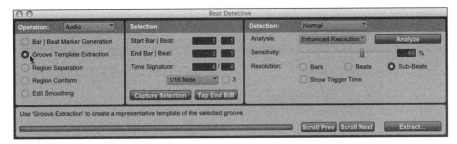

Figure 4.45 Groove Template Extraction mode.

4. Click the Capture Selection button. The Start and End Bar | Beat locations should match the selection in the Edit window.

5. Click the Analyze button.

6. Raise the Sensitivity slider until most or all of the transients have a beat trigger (shown in Figure 4.46).

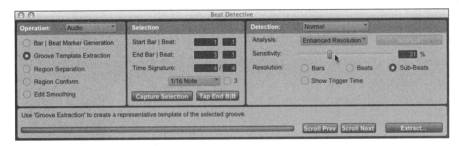

Figure 4.46 Raise the Sensitivity slider until beat triggers appear.

7. Click the Extract button. The Extract Groove Template dialog box should appear.

8. Click the Save to Groove Clipboard button found in the Extract Groove Template dialog box.

The groove template in now temporarily stored on the Groove Clipboard. You can now apply this groove without having to mess about with storing files and whatnot. (Although, fear not, the next example does cover how to store groove templates.)

Tightening Tracks

Tightening all tracks in the intro and Section A with the groove template:

1. Make sure all the tracks are locked to the ticks timebase and that you have the Elastic Audio plug-in enabled (refer to Chapter 2 for information regarding timebases and Elastic Audio plug-ins).

2. Enable the All edit group by clicking on <ALL> in the Groups pane (shown in Figure 4.47).

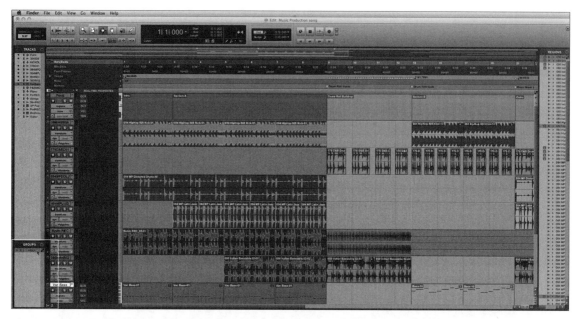

Figure 4.47   Highlight the <ALL> group in the Groups list to group all tracks.

3.   Select the intro and Section A regions on the Form track. With the <ALL> group enabled, all tracks are selected.

4.   Press Option+3 on the numeric keypad to open the Event Operations window.

5.   Select Quantize from the pop-up menu at the top of the window.

6.   Choose Elastic Audio Events from the What to Quantize pop-up menu.

7.   Choose Groove Clipboard from the Quantize Grid pop-up menu.

8.   In the Options section, check Timing and set it to 100%.

9.   If your Event Operations window looks like Figure 4.48, click Apply.

10.   Disable the <ALL> group by clicking on it in the Groups list.

The tightening effects on the regions are subtle, and it may be difficult to hear a specific instance of the tightening actually occurring. If you take a step back and listen to the whole piece, you will notice how it just feels more together. The next example, however, is anything but subtle.

Because you have the power to extract the groove of any audio or MIDI recording, there is nothing stopping you from importing a loop that you like the feel of (but not necessarily the audio quality) for the sole purpose of extracting the groove and applying it to your entire session.

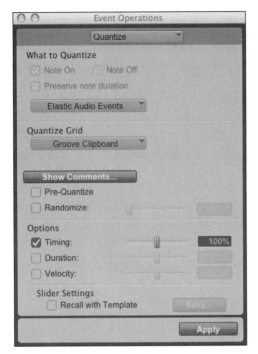

Figure 4.48   The Event Operations window (quantizing a groove template).

Importing Loops

In this next example, you will import a loop from the Pro Tools loops collection, extract its groove, and apply it to all the tracks in the outro.

Importing the 91 R&B Drumtrack 06.wav audio file into your session:

1. Open the Workspace.

2. Click the Find button (the magnifying glass icon), type "91 R&B Drumtrack 06.wav" in the Name field, and click Search (see Figure 4.49).

3. Drag the file from the Workspace to the Tracks list. A new track should automatically be created with the region at its start (see Figure 4.50).

4. Close the Workspace browser.

5. Enable the Rhythmic Elastic Audio plug-in on this track (see Chapter 2 if you forget how to do this).

6. With the TCE Trim tool, stretch the loop so that it is exactly two bars long.

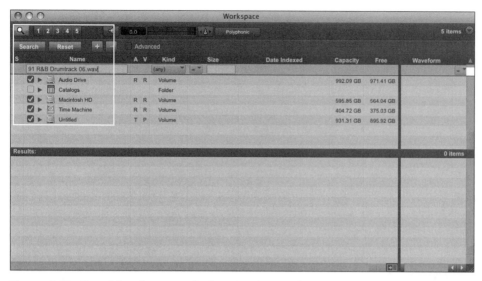

Figure 4.49   Searching for an audio loop in the Workspace.

Figure 4.50   Dragging an audio file from the Workspace to the Tracks list will automatically create a new track.

Extracting the Groove Loop and Deleting the Track

Next you will extract the groove as you did with the Hip Hop Kick loop. Only this time, you will store the loop in the groove template library.

Extracting a groove from 91 R&B Drumtrack 06 region and creating a custom template:

1. Follow the steps of the previous process in which you created a groove template from the 084 Hip Hop Kick loop to extract the groove of this region as you did with the Hip Hop loop.

2. Click the Save to Disk button in the Extract Groove Template dialog box (shown in Figure 4.51).

Figure 4.51 The Extract Groove Template dialog box.

3. Create a new folder and name it "RnB Grooves."

4. Name the template "91 RnB Drumtrack Swing" and click Save (shown in Figure 4.52).

Now that you have extracted the groove from the 91 R&B Drumtrack 06 region, you no longer need the track in your session.

Deleting the 091 R&B Drumtrack 06 track from your session:

1. Select the track by clicking on its name in the Edit or Mix window.

2. Choose Track > Delete or right-click on the track name and choose Delete.

Next, you can apply this groove to any and all tracks in your session. For the purpose of this tutorial, you will change the groove of the outro to have the swing feel of the template you just created.

Figure 4.52 Saving an extracted groove to your groove library.

Applying the New Groove Template

Applying the new groove template to audio events in the outro:

1. Select the outro regions on the Form track. With the <ALL> group enabled, all tracks are selected.

2. Press Option+3 to open the Event Operations window.

3. Choose Quantize from the Operation pull-down menu.

4. Choose 91 RnB Drumtrack Swing from the Quantize Grid pull-down menu.

5. Click Apply.

6. Once again, disable the <ALL> group by clicking on it in the Groups list.

Since the loop you are importing has a deep swing feel, you will undoubtedly see and hear the effects of the groove quantize.

Tutorial 18: Writing Snapshot Automation to Change Plug-In Settings

Pro Tools automation is a vast subject, and it seems to have more features with each release. As it stands now, there are few (if any) automation systems that offer the flexibility and power that are available within Pro Tools. Rather than attempt to address all aspects of this topic with moderate success, this tutorial covers a single area in a more complete fashion, specifically snapshot automation.

Many people comment when working with virtual instruments (and other real-time plug-ins) that there is no way for plug-ins to automatically switch between presets at a specific point in time. Although you can't select a preset automatically, Pro Tools can automate all of the parameters that the plug-in setting recalls. The result is the same, except you have the added flexibility of modifying the automation on a parameter-by-parameter basis after the snapshots have been written.

Automation Basics

In order to take advantage of snapshot automation, you should know how Pro Tools automation works. When a track is initially created, it contains automation playlists for Volume, Mute, and Pan. If a send is added to the track, Send Level, Send Mute, and Send Pan automation playlists are automatically created.

Plug-ins, on the other hand, are treated somewhat differently. When a plug-in is added to a track, automation playlists are not automatically created. This is due to the fact that the number of parameters can vary greatly from one plug-in to the next. Furthermore, an excessive number of unnecessary playlists can have an adverse effect on system performance while adding no real value to the session.

So if you want to automate a plug-in parameter, the parameter needs to be automation enabled in the actual plug-in window. Once a parameter is enabled, the automation playlist will appear in the track's View Selector menu.

TIP: Tracks can be in one of five automation modes: Read, Write, Touch, Latch, or Off. By default a track is in Read mode. This tutorial assumes that your tracks are in Read mode unless otherwise specified. If you are unsure which automation mode your tracks are in or how to switch the mode to Read, use Figure 4.58 as your guide. This figure illustrates where the Track Automation selector can be found in the Edit window.

Enabling a Plug-In Parameter for Automation

Enabling a plug-in parameter for automation:

1. Click on the Vacuum plug-in insert to open the Vacuum plug-in window.

2. Click the Plug-In Automation button (shown in Figure 4.53) to open the Plug-In Automation window.

3. Select the Master Bypass parameter.

4. Click the Add button.

5. If your Plug-In Automation dialog box looks like Figure 4.54, click OK.

You should notice that the color of the word Bypass in the Bypass button has changed from white to green. This tells you that this parameter is now responding to its automation playlist.

Figure 4.53   The Plug-In Automation button.

If you play your session and click the Master Bypass button, you will find that it doesn't behave any differently than before. Essentially, this is because there is no automation written for this parameter. Now is a good time to look at what is happening behind the scenes so you will better understand one of the most misunderstood (and potentially frustrating) aspects of Pro Tools automation.

Showing the Master Bypass Automation Playlist

Showing the Master Bypass automation playlist for the Vacuum plug-in:

1.   Click the Track View selector.

2.   Choose (fx a) Vacuum > Master Bypass (see Figure 4.55).

     —OR—

3.   Control+Command+click the Bypass button in the Vacuum Plug-In window.

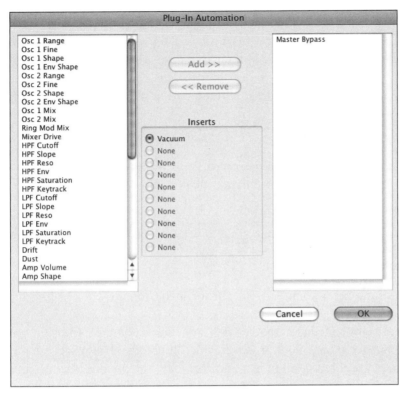

Figure 4.54   The Plug-In Automation window.

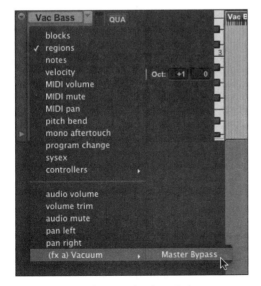

Figure 4.55   The Track View Selector menu.

With the Vacuum plug-in window and the Vac Bass Master Bypass automation playlist in the Edit window showing, click the Bypass button a couple of times. Do you notice how the automation playlist updates to reflect the current status of the parameter? This is a convenience. If only the initial value is preset, Pro Tools will update that value on the fly (without writing any automation). This is not only true for plug-ins, but for all automation playlists (including Volume, Pan, and Mute).

Adding an Automation Breakpoint

Adding a single additional point to a playlist will prevent Pro Tools from updating its status on the fly. Instead, you will be required to edit the automation playlist directly.

Using the Grabber tool to add an automation breakpoint:

1.   Select the Grabber tool in the Edit window.

2.   Click anywhere in the Vac Bass track playlist to add an automation breakpoint.

3.   The specific location of the breakpoint is irrelevant for this example.

With another automation breakpoint added (see Figure 4.56), try clicking on the Bypass button in the Vacuum plug-in window once more. Now, it is behaving differently. The playlist is not updating. You can bypass the plug-in, but as soon as you press Play, the plug-in becomes un-bypassed.

Figure 4.56 Adding another automation breakpoint will "lock" the playlist from being adjusted in Read mode.

Although this may seem frustrating, especially if you are trying to temporarily mute a track that contains some mute automation, Pro Tools is just doing what it is supposed to do. In a fit of rage, you may be inclined to just go crazy and delete all automation break points on the track playlist. Although this does have the short-term upside of allowing you to control the parameter again, you would lose all of the automation that you painstaking placed on the track.

Disabling Automation

If you really don't want Pro Tools to respond to automation, there are a few places where it can be disabled—depending on the amount of automation you want to turn off.

First up, you can turn off automation for the entire session—every track and every parameter.

Turning off automation for the session:

1. Choose Window > Automation or press Command+4 on the numeric keypad.

2. In the Automation Enable window, click the Suspend button (see Figure 4.57).

Note that the Bypass button in the Vacuum plug-in window changed back from green to white. This is Pro Tools' way of letting you know that it is no longer responding to automation playlists.

Figure 4.57 Clicking Suspend in the Automation Enable window will turn off automation for the entire session.

You may, however, find this a little excessive for this particular situation. If so, you can simply click on the Suspend button in the Automation Enable window again to unsuspend the session automation.

There may be times when you want to listen to some tracks being automated while the track you are working on is suspended. By changing the track's automation mode, you can effectively suspend automation on a track-by-track basis.

Turning off the Vac Bass's track automation:

1.   Click the Automation Mode selector.

2.   Choose Off (see Figure 4.58).

Figure 4.58   The Track Automation Mode menu.

Again, the Bypass button changes from green to white. The good news is that you can now adjust any and all track or plug-in settings on this track without fear of the parameters you are adjusting switching back when you press Play. The bad news is that the track will not respond to any automation playlists. For instance, disabling automation for the track will allow you to control the mute status, but you no longer will hear the panning and volume automation.

Disabling a Specific Automation Playlist

Switch the Vac Bass's automation mode back to Auto Read. In this case, you will be best suited to just disable a specific automation playlist.

Suspending an automation playlist of a single parameter:

1.   Make sure the (fx a) Vacuum Master Bypass playlist is still showing on the Vac Bass track.

2.   Command+click on the Track View selector.

The Track View selector will turn gray with italic text (see Figure 4.59), and the text in the Bypass button will once again turn from green to white.

Figure 4.59 Command+clicking on the Track View selector will disable the automation playlist.

Command+click on the Track View selector to unsuspend the parameter automation. That should do it in terms of a basic understanding of what is happening behind the scenes with automation playlists and how you can disable them.

Creating Plug-in Settings and a Cautionary Tale

Now that some of the confusing aspects of automation are out of the way, you can turn your attention to having the Vacuum instrument change its setting for the Section B area of the session.

Chapter 2 covered how to create and save plug-in settings. It is always a good idea to save plug-in settings for each of the states that you expect the plug-in to switch to over the course of the session. This means that should save the modified 07 Juno 106 Bass preset.

Selecting and saving Vacuum plug-in settings to the session plug-in settings folder:

1. Save the modified version of 07 Juno 106 Bass as MP Bass 1 to the Session's Settings folder.

2. Choose another plug-in preset from the Librarian menu > 2 Bass (such as 07 Massive).

3. Modify it any way that you see fit.

4. Save the modified version to the Session's Settings folder as "MP Bass 2."

5. Switch to the MP Bass 1 plug-in setting.

At this point you should have two unique bass plug-in settings available in the Librarian menu > Session's Settings folder (see Figure 4.60).

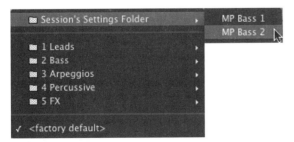

Figure 4.60 Vacuum's Librarian menu showing two bass session plug-in settings.

The next step is to enable all of the plug-in parameters. Although you can repeat the steps that describe how to enable the Master Bypass, there is a much quicker way. You simply Control+Option+Command+click on the Plug-in Automation button.

TIP: If you find yourself using plug-in automation extensively, you can have Pro Tools auto-enable all plug-in parameters when a plug-in is added to a track. Choose Setup > Preferences, and then click on the Mixing tab. In that window, check the Plug-in Controls Default to Auto-Enable checkbox.

Instantly, you should see a tiny little green square appear next to each parameter, letting you know that they are all enabled for automation. Technically, you are all ready to start automating, and you might be feeling a little excited. This also happens to be where things have a habit of going horribly wrong, thus killing all of the enthusiasm built up.

Beware and Be Wise

Take a moment and read this cautionary tale, as its lesson may help you avoid some potholes that are commonly associated with snapshot automation. Our tale starts out at the very same situation you are in now. The fictitious Pro Tools operator (let's call him Billy) has a Vacuum plug-in set to the MP Bass 1 setting, and as a result, all of its parameter automation playlists are set to play MP Bass 1. When Billy presses the Play button, everything sounds as it always did.

Now he wants to use a new plug-in setting for Section B, and Billy can't wait to hear how it sounds. So he selects Section B on the Vac Bass track, changes the plug-in setting to MP Bass 2, and then proceeds to write some automation. He listens back to Section B, and it sounds better than he had hoped. So he presses Return to listen to his session from the start. Suddenly, Billy notices something wrong... now MP Bass 2 is playing in the intro and in Section A. Initially, he thinks that it is easy enough to correct... or is it? He selects the MP Bass 1 setting from the Librarian menu, but it keeps jumping back to the MP Bass 2 sound each time playback is started. Not knowing how to fix the problem, Billy feels defeated and turns off all automation for the existing track, creates a new instrument track with a Vacuum plug-in (set to MP Bass 2), and copies all of the MIDI data in Section B from the Vac Bass track to the Vac Bass 2 track. He never works with snapshot automation again.

What happened to Billy is tragic—his impression of snapshot automation is corrupted, he is feeling frustrated, and now his session is bloated unnecessarily. Furthermore, all of this could have been avoided if he had not forgotten one little step.

If you have experienced this little drama, you are certainly not alone. Although it is frustrating and seems unintuitive, it isn't difficult to understand what is happening to cause this behavior. Remember when there was no automation on the Master Bypass playlist? When you adjusted the Bypass plug-in, it affected the entire playlist for the duration of the session. This is the heart of what caused so many problems for Billy.

Because there was no initial automation on the track, when he switched from MP Bass 1 to MP Bass 2, the entire playlist for each parameter was updated to the new value for the duration of the session, regardless of whether there is a selection. This in and of itself isn't a big deal to correct because the playlist can be updated again by switching the plug-in setting back to MP Bass 1.

The problem occurs when automation is written when the MP Bass 2 setting is active. Now there are additional automation points added to the parameter playlists. Just like when you added a point to the Master Bypass playlist, Pro Tools will no longer update the parameter playlists, thus Billy kept hearing MP Bass 2 after he pressed Play, even though he switched back to MP Bass 1.

This undoubtedly creates a great deal of stress and disappointment. It can, however be avoided by keeping one thing in mind—always remember to write your "default" parameter setting to automation playlists first. That way, you can be assured that the plug-in will always return to the appropriate settings.

In short, if you want Vacuum to switch to MP Bass 2 only for the duration of Section B, you must first write some automation breakpoints as MP Bass 1 to lock it in as the track's default patch.

Controlling What Is "Written"

As you might have guessed, writing automation can have a serious impact on your workflow. That is why it is vital to be diligent in controlling what information is written to automation playlists. Much like suspending automation, you can prevent writing on a couple of different levels.

First off, you can write-enable or -disable playlists for the entire session through the Automation Enable window. In this tutorial, you write automation only for Vacuum, which is a plug-in. Although it's technically optional, you should disable the ability to write any other type of automation; not only does this prevent you from inadvertently overwriting an existing automation pass, but also prevents parameters from unintentionally "locking" playlists into a default position.

Write-enabling the plug-in automation for the session only:

1. Choose Window > Automation or press Command+4 on the numeric keypad.

2. In the Write Enable section of Automation Enable window, toggle each of the write-enable buttons so the Plug-In button is red and the rest are gray.

Now the session will only be able to write plug-in parameters. This window doesn't provide you with any means to prevent a specific plug-in from getting overwritten. To prevent this, you can place a plug-in into Automation Safe mode. You will learn how to do this after writing some automation into the Vac Bass track.

On a side note, writing automation in real-time directly to tracks is usually controlled by the track's current automation mode. This, however, doesn't apply to the Write Automation command in the Edit menu, which will write automation parameters to a selection on any track regardless of the automation mode (the Write Enables in the Automation window must still be active, however).

Ready, Set, Snapshot!

Although it might seem like a really long preamble to get to this point, you will find that there isn't anything especially complicated with actually writing snapshot automation. With all of the preparations you took in the previous sections, you are set to write in all of the automation while bypassing any potholes that could have created problems. So without further ado, let's start writing some automation!

Remember the little story that was presented earlier in the tutorial? Writing the default plug-in parameters is the first order of business. In this case, it means writing the MP Bass 1 parameters specifically.

Writing the MP Bass 1 plug-in parameters to the Vac Bass track:

1. Triple-click on the Vac Bass track. All regions on that track should be selected.

2. Choose Edit > Automation > Write to All Enabled (shown in Figure 4.61), or press Option+Command+/ to write the plug-in parameters.

Now you wrote in some static, default parameters. The next step is to snapshot in the MP Bass 2 setting for Section B.

Writing the MP Bass 2 plug-in parameters to Section B of the Vac Bass track:

1. Select Section B on the Form track.

2. Press P or ; (semicolon) to move the selection to the Vac Bass track.

3. In the Vacuum plug-in, choose the Librarian menu > Session's Settings folder > MP Bass 2.

4. Choose Edit > Automation > Write to All Enabled, or press Option+Command+/ to write the plug-in parameters.

If you play the track, you should notice that all of the parameters change to MP Bass 2 for the duration of Section B and change back to the setting of MP Bass 1 at the outro. You should also note that the plug-in's setting name *doesn't* change; only the parameters in the actual plug-in change.

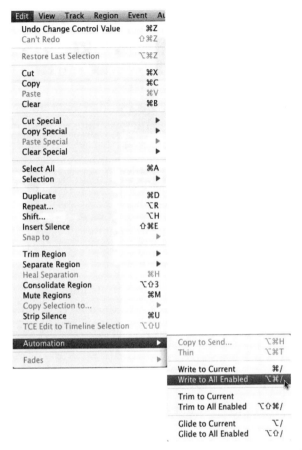

Figure 4.61 The Write to All Enabled option is available from the Edit menu.

Another way to verify that the automation write was successful is to Control+Command+click various parameters and look at the Vac Bass track in the Edit window. You should see a change in the parameter automation playlists for the duration of Section B (shown in Figure 4.62).

Lastly, if you are happy with how the Vacuum bass automates, you should place it in Automation Safe mode. This will protect all automation playlists that are associated with this plug-in

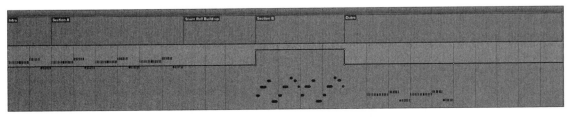

Figure 4.62 Automation playlists reflect the changes when snapshots change between presets.

from being overwritten. To place it in Automation Safe mode, you click on the Safe button in the plug-in heading of the Vacuum plug-in.

Tutorial 19: Processing with Real-Time Plug-Ins

One of the greatest additions to Pro Tools 8 is the inclusion of all the AIR real-time plug-ins. In Chapter 2, you looked at a couple of the virtual instrument plug-ins; now it is time to look at some real-time effects.

Most of the joy in working with these plug-ins is discovering how different they can make your recordings or virtual instruments sound. To that end, please feel free to experiment with them to your heart's content.

If you want some guidance, however, use the following sections as a starting point.

Vocalizing the Boom Rec Track

By applying the Talkbox plug-in to the Boom track, you can turn a standard drum-machine–sounding track into something more interesting. Experiment with automating the Vowel parameter to get even more interesting effects.

Vocalizing the Boom drums:

1. On the Boom Rec track insert, choose Harmonic > AIR Talkbox.

2. From the AIR Talkbox Librarian menu, choose 13 Mouth Percussion.

Automating the Vowel parameter in the AIR Talkbox plug-in:

1. Control+Option+click the Vowel parameter to automation-enable it.

2. Control+Command+click the Vowel parameter in the plug-in window to show the Vowel automation playlist on the track in the Edit window.

3. Set the Grid to $^1/_{16}$ note (see Figure 4.63).

4. Select the Random Pencil tool (see Figure 4.64).

5. Click and drag the Boom Rec track from Bar 1 through Bar 8 to draw random values for the Vowel parameter (shown in Figure 4.65).

For an added challenge, try to increase the formant parameter linearly over the drum roll.

Pulsating the Pad Rec Track

AIR Filter Gate is a great plug-in for adding timbre control or a rhythmic quality to your tracks. In this example, you'll use it to add a pulsing sound to the Pad track.

Figure 4.63 Setting the grid in the Edit window.

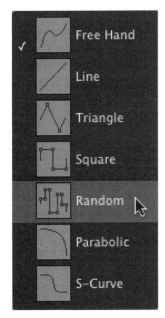

Figure 4.64 Click and hold the Pencil tool to access all of its options.

Pulsating the Pad Rec track:

1. On the Pad Rec insert, choose Modulation > AIR Filter Gate.

2. From the AIR Filter Gate Librarian menu, choose 24 Rhythmic Pattern.

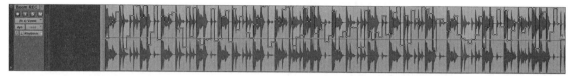

Figure 4.65 Click and drag to draw random automation values.

You can add even more expression by automating the Gate parameters (primarily Hold and Release).

Thickening the Strings Rec Track

The default strings are a little thin. The AIR Phaser goes a long way toward adding depth and interest to a rather unremarkable sound.

Thickening the Strings Rec track:

1. On the Strings Rec insert, choose Modulation > AIR Phaser.

2. From the AIR Filter Gate Librarian menu, choose 01 Long and Wide Phaser.

As I mentioned earlier, this is really just a starting point. With so many plug-ins, each having parameters that can be automated, you can go a long time without duplicating the same sound.

Tutorial 20: Moving and Storing Sessions

Although the subject of this tutorial might seem boring at first, it could very well be one of the most important tutorials of the book. This is because all of the creativity in the world won't be able to help you if you can't deliver the session to the client or studio.

In my tenure as a teacher, I have seen many amazing students brought to their knees when they found that the project that they worked so hard on was missing files when they transferred it to another studio for final evaluation.

So if you are working with other people or studios, please take this advice. If you only have time to work one tutorial into your repertoire at the moment, make it this one!

Cleaning Up the Regions List

Before getting in the nitty-gritty details regarding session archival, it is a good idea to clean up the Regions list a little bit. Tons of unused regions get created as a result of all the editing and compositing you do. Every once in a while, it is a good idea to clean up the Regions list in order to keep it manageable.

Removing unused regions from the Regions list:

1. Choose Select > Unused from the Regions list pop-up menu (see Figure 4.66) or press Command+Shift+U to select any unused regions in the Regions list.

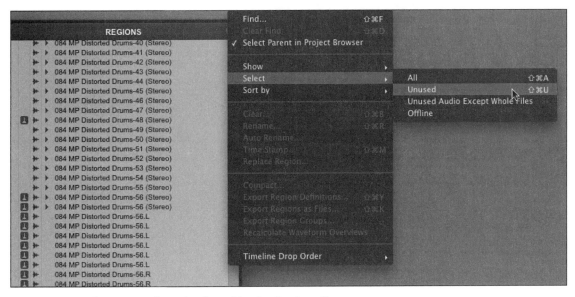

Figure 4.66   Select Unused can be found in the Regions list pop-up menu.

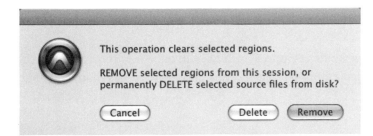

Figure 4.67   The Clear dialog box, where you remove any unused regions.

2.   Choose Clear from the Regions list pop-up menu or press Command+Shift+B to bring up the Clear dialog box (see Figure 4.67).

3.   Click Remove.

Wow! Instant Regions list cleanup!

Moving Sessions Between Systems

All of the different flavors of Pro Tools (LE, HD, and M-Powered) across the Macintosh and Windows platforms are compatible. This means that you can have a tracking session in an HD studio with a Mac, take it home and edit it on your PC with the M-Powered version, and then bring it to a different studio for mixing. The session will open perfectly well in all of these cases—provided you take the proper steps to ensure that all of the media moves with the session. Furthermore, Pro Tools will open a session even if it cannot find all of the media that pertains to it.

Online and Offline Regions

Online regions are any regions that Pro Tools can find. In most cases, Pro Tools should have all audio regions online. If, for some reason, you open a session and Pro Tools can't locate all of the media, it will present you with the Missing Files dialog box, shown in Figure 4.68. You can click one of the Relink buttons, and Pro Tools will do an extensive search in the background, but it is always better just to avoid that mess entirely with some easy preventative measures.

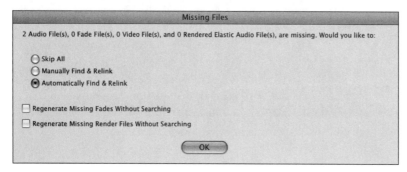

Figure 4.68 The Missing Files dialog box can help you in a pinch.

If you do end up needing to relink some audio regions, Pro Tools will tell you if those regions are on the timeline or just missing from the Regions list. Figure 4.69 shows two icons that will either be green or red.

Figure 4.69 You have offline regions if either of these icons is red.

If they are both green, all regions are online. If the one on the right is red, you are missing files in the Regions list, but they are not on the timeline, thus it shouldn't affect how the session plays back. If both are red, you are missing audio from the timeline, and your session may sound differently than you expect. You can tell which regions are offline because their names are italicized and there is no waveform (see Figure 4.70).

Managing Files in Project Browser

The Project browser is instrumental in helping you keep track of all your media. In most cases, your media should be in the Session folder, but with multiple record drives (discussed in Chapter 3), you can have audio spread out. The Path field of the Project browser shows you where Pro Tools expects to find each piece of media.

Offline Regions

Figure 4.70   Boom REC_02-01 and Guitar_03-12 are both offline regions.

Displaying the Project browser and creating a custom view:

1.   Choose Window > Project to display the Project browser.

2.   Scroll the second pane to show the Path field (see Figure 4.71).

If Pro Tools can't find a piece of media, it will appear offline, and you have the option of manually relinking to it. Manual relinking allows a little more flexibility in regards to determining how Pro Tools identifies valid media. This could prove useful when you are in a bind.

In a perfect world, Pro Tools will find every required piece of media based on the filename and unique ID. Things happen, however, and there might be times when the name or ID is no longer valid. For instance, someone might inadvertently rename a required audio file within the operating system. If either of these pieces of information is invalid, Pro Tools will not automatically link to the media. You can, however, override this option with the Manual Relink function.

Manually finding and relinking offline media:

1.   Right-click an offline region and choose Relink Selected. This will open the Relink window.

2.   In the top pane of the Relink window, select all valid drives or folders that might possibly contain the media.

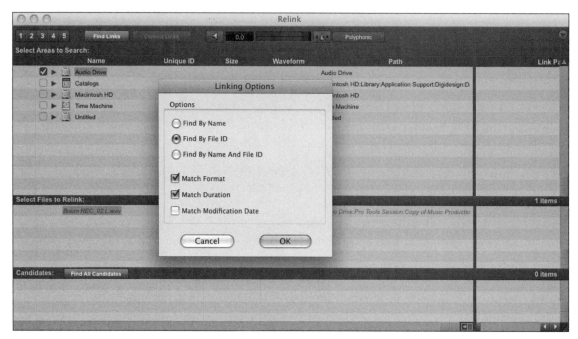

Figure 4.71 The Path field in the Project browser tells you where Pro Tools expects to find each piece of media.

3. Click the Find Links button to open the Linking Options dialog box (see Figure 4.72).

4. Select the appropriate options and click OK.

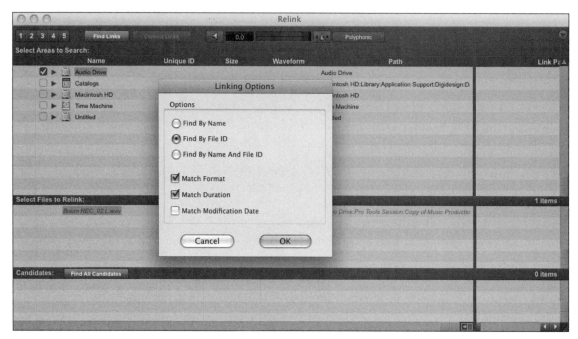

Figure 4.72 Selecting Find by File ID is a great way to locate a file if you suspect it might have been renamed.

Using Save Copy In

If your session is completely online and you are looking to archive or move it to another storage device or computer, it is a good idea to perform a Save Copy In operation to ensure that all of the media is transferred properly to the new volume.

Performing a Save Copy In operation to store the session on a new volume:

1.   Choose File > Save Copy In to open the Save Session Copy dialog box (see Figure 4.73).

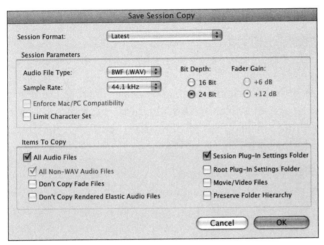

Figure 4.73 The Save Session Copy dialog box allows you to copy all session-related files to a single drive for easy archival.

2.   In the Items to Copy section, check all relevant boxes.

3.   Click OK.

4.   Choose the volume and folder where you want the session to be saved.

5.   Name the session something appropriate.

6.   Click Save.

Pro Tools will proceed to collect and copy all of the relevant media to the new volume.

In addition to archiving your session data, you can also use Save Copy In to create versions of your session that are compatible with older versions of Pro Tools.

Summary

In this chapter, you learned how to make significant changes to your session through the use of editing techniques, real-time plug-ins, and automation.

Event operations allow you to change or restore note attributes, whereas real-time properties allow changes without any commitments.

By using Beat Detective to create groove templates, you can tighten all of the tracks in your session while keeping the original feel.

You also learned about snapshot automation. By using snapshots, you can make more efficient use of your virtual instruments and keep your sessions running smoothly.

Lastly, you saw how the Save Copy In operation can collect all of your media and copy it to a central location. From there, you can archive it on a tape backup or DVD, transfer it to a removable disk in order to bring it to a different studio, or even create versions of your session that are compatible with older versions of Pro Tools.

Wrapping Up and Moving On

Although this chapter marks the end of this book, it hopefully also marks a starting point for how you handle your projects with Pro Tools. As stated in the Introduction, these tutorials are designed not only to show you how to do things in Pro Tools, but also to explain why these processes are in place and why you should know and use them.

There are many instances where I have pulled from my experiences as a Pro Tools user, as a teacher, and even as a witness to the many pitfalls of novice users, to provide context for the features described in this book. Given that everyone comes to Pro Tools with a slightly different set of experiences, you are also encouraged to answer the "why" question in your own way. You will have a better chance of incorporating the concepts of this book if you determine why they are important to you.

In many ways, this book is just a group of starts for the ideas that are contained within. It is my hope that these "starts" set your creativity flowing with ways to build on the lessons learned here. By making these tutorials your own, you will find before long that you are using Pro Tools with a certain efficiency and fluidity that wasn't there before. Good luck!

Index